See Me
Hear Me
Know Me

See Me

for who I am,

Hear Me

so you will understand,

Know Me

and my love for you.

Randy & Paula White

Without Walls International Church

TAMPA, FLORIDA

Printed in the United States of America

ISBN: 0-9712650-0-3

Pastors Randy and Paula White
Without Walls International Church
2511 Without Walls International Place
Tampa, FL 33607

CONTENTS

INTRODUCTION

The wedding day has come…and gone. The rice has been thrown, photos have been taken, gifts are unwrapped, the rented limousine had just driven off into the sunset, and you are standing alone with the one to whom you have vowed to share a lifetime. Are you ready for the journey beyond the veil?

When Randy and I were newly wed, we had preconceived ideas of what a marriage was all about. We were reminded of a story about a farmer who had just taken a wife. Her heart would beat, pitter pat, at the mere mention of his name. Every time they so much as kissed, the butterflies in her stomach went wild! She thought he was the next best thing to sliced bread. They were "so in love."

Like most newlyweds, they didn't have a lot of money. They didn't own a family car, but they did own a donkey. One day, while riding their donkey up a steep mountain road, the donkey stumbled. The farmer dismounted, leaving his bride sitting atop the animal. He walked over to face the donkey, pointed his finger, and said, "One!" Then he remounted the donkey and rode on.

The bride didn't know what to think of this strange communication between her husband and his donkey. She had never seen this side of him before.

They proceeded up the mountain road and the donkey stumbled again. Once more, the farmer dismounted and staring the animal in the face, he shook his finger and said, "Two!"

After a short pause, the farmer got back on the donkey and proceeded on the journey. Further down the road, the donkey stopped dead in its tracks. The farmer dismounted—only this time he took his bride with him. Carefully aiming his rifle, he shot the donkey right between the eyes.

The blushing bride was shocked at her husband's behavior and became hysterical. "I can't believe it! Look what you've done! You've just shot the donkey! Are you crazy?" she wailed.

At that moment, the farmer turned to his wife, pointed his finger at her, and said, "One!"

Whether you're about to be married, are a newlywed, or have many years of marriage under your belt, you may have counted past two by now. Please join us as we take a candid, reality-based look at marriage and all that is required to make it last! Written for couples and singles alike, the dynamic keys to commitment and communication we share in these pages are designed to bring joy and fulfillment to your marriage. Remember, your wedding is an event, but your marriage is a lifetime achievement!

With all our love,

Randy and Paula

one

HIS NEEDS/ HER NEEDS: APPRECIATING THE DIFFERENCES

Paula: Throughout the history of the world, the responsibility for original sin has been blamed on Eve, largely because Adam did what all of us try to do. We run and tell on someone else so we won't get the blame. Adam ran to God and said, "This woman you gave me brought me that apple, and I did eat it" (see Genesis 3:12). Women have gotten the blame ever since.

Adam hadn't recognized his need for partnership. He was in paradise. He was happy. He thought everything was going well. Then . . . *the Lord God said, It is not good that the man should be alone; I will make him an help meet for him. . . . And the Lord God caused a deep sleep to fall upon Adam, and he slept: and he took one of his ribs, and closed up the flesh instead thereof; and the rib, which the Lord God had taken from man, made he a woman, and brought her unto the man* (Genesis 2:18,21,22).

Randy: We must understand that before God ever gave Adam the woman, He had formed Adam from the dirt and assigned him to till the ground. In other words, He gave man a job first. Man was birthed into *productivity,* while woman was birthed into *relationship.*

There are major differences in males and females, and people who want to have a successful marriage must understand and appreciate those differences. Man was birthed into productivity and position. God gave him something to do first. As a result, men get worth and value out of doing something.

A WOMAN SEES HER VALUE THROUGH RELATIONSHIP, WHILE A MAN SEES HIS VALUE THROUGH PRODUCTIVITY.

One of the key issues I encounter in counseling men is the frustration they feel when they're not working or unable to provide for their family. Working and providing give men a sense of what life is all about. It's extremely depressing to a man when he cannot provide for his family, because God put it inside a man to be the breadwinner.

Paula: We grow frustrated with each other because we don't understand the differences between men and women. God made us to *complete*—not to *compete* with—one another. It is imperative for us to understand that together we make the picture whole. Together we complete the puzzle.

Many women fail to understand that men were born to produce and that the source of a man's fulfillment comes from what he does. If you ever want to create a marriage disaster, just start to attack what your husband does or his ability to provide. Never, ever do that or you have just tied a suicidal noose around your neck. A wife should never criticize her husband's ability to do or to perform.

Eve, on the other hand, was taken from Adam's rib and birthed into relationship. She was created to be a wife. Now, think about that. She woke up a married woman! Can you imagine? We give Eve such a hard time, but when she woke up, she heard, "Honey, get me the grits . . . and where are my socks?" No wonder the girlfriend went on a long walk and lent her ear to Satan.

She had no books, no Dr. Dobson, no Gary Smalley, no Randy and Paula White to tell her how to make it work. Just, "Honey, get me a glass of water." "Baby, what are we going to have for breakfast today?"

She was birthed into relationship.

EVE . . . WAS CREATED TO BE A WIFE. NOW, THINK ABOUT THAT. SHE WOKE UP A MARRIED WOMAN!

If you ask a man who he is, he'll tell you what he does. "I'm the pastor of Without Walls International Church in Tampa, Florida." "I'm the vice president of whatever company."

If you ask a woman who she is, she'll say, "I'm the mother of Johnnie and Suzie. I'm the wife of Randy." A woman sees her value through relationship, while a man sees his value through productivity.

Randy: **The fall of man only compounded and magnified the existing situations and conditions. The consequences of sin** impacted Adam and Eve in unique ways. For the man, the consequence was less productive ground, with thorns and thistles, requiring "painful toil" and the "sweat of his brow." Notice that the consequence affected his work, his *productivity.*

Paula: But for Eve, in addition to taking on the pain of childbirth, the consequence of the sinful fall struck at her *relationship.* Genesis 3:16 says, . . . *thy desire shall be to thy husband, and he shall rule over thee.*

WHY ARE ALL MEN "LIKE THAT"?

Randy: Many mothers warn their daughters that all men have one-track minds. "All they ever think about is sex, sex, sex!" If this is true, then why are males so obsessively driven by sexual desire? One of the main reasons is that men are sight-stimulated. Let's just get it out in the open and deal with it. We think when we get married and start having a sexual relationship with our wife that our lust or desire for women is going to be satisfied and we'll never have a problem with it again. Wrong! It is not going to go away.

I've often had teenagers and young men come to me saying, "Pastor, my hormones are just bouncing off my bones. There must be something wrong with me! Every woman I see . . . I mean . . . you wouldn't believe it. Why am I doing this? What is going on?"

God placed in men a desire for women. What you must understand is that you have to harness that drive and bring those desires under submission through the power of the Holy Spirit. That's why the apostle Paul said, . . . *I die daily* (1 Corinthians 15:31).

I've often told Paula, "I'm one step away from sinning. I can make a choice today that I don't want to remain in a faithful, monogamous relationship any longer and walk away. I must choose this relationship. I have chosen this relationship."

I understand some of the struggles of single men and husbands. As a man and a pastor, I know the things that we struggle with. We can try to sweep our thoughts and feelings under the rug all we want to, but it won't work. I deal with the same struggles, so I know what I'm talking about.

You can walk by a magazine rack and see Pamela Anderson on the cover of *Playboy*, flip through a few pages, and you're in trouble. Why? Because men are sight-stimulated. You love your wife. You can pretend to be Mr. Super-spiritual, a high-minded, never-think-of-sex, Christian man, but God made you to desire women, and He made you to be sight-stimulated.

Matthew 6:22 in *The Message* expresses it well, *"Your eyes are windows into your body. If you open your eyes wide in wonder and belief, your body fills up with light. If you live squinty-eyed in greed and distrust, your body is a dark cellar. If you pull the blinds on your windows, what a dark life you will have!"*

This is why pornography doesn't have the same effect on women that it has on men. I met a pastor recently who has written a book on the subject of shame. He was the pastor of a successful church, but one night at a hotel in a city where he was scheduled to be a conference speaker, he randomly flipped through the TV channels and noticed there was a pornographic movie playing. He lingered too long on that channel and eventually watched the whole movie.

He tells the whole story in his book, but the result was that seven years later this man lived out everything his eyes saw that night in the movie. He was with prostitutes. He was with strippers. He was going into adult bookstores in disguise on Saturday nights and preaching in the pulpit every Sunday.

Paula: Let me point out that a story like this is so frightening and threatening to women. A wife thinks that if her man looks, he automatically loves. But try to understand that a man can give his eye—even his body—and not give his heart away. The moment you begin to comprehend that he can look without loving, the threat is reduced. Just because he may notice and be momentarily attracted to that woman on television or on the sidewalk doesn't mean that he doesn't love you.

It's important that you understand this because if you don't, you'll become nagging, jealous, and possessive. You'll try to put him in a box, and guess what? Human nature is going to get out of the box. You cannot be jealous and obsessive and try to put a man into "prison" because he's looking around. You must realize and understand that as a man, he was created this way.

A friend of ours told us about his struggle with this very thing in mid-life. Because he and his wife enjoyed such a great relationship, he felt free to confide in her, "I think that woman is beautiful, and she took my eye." This woman knew her husband well, and she clearly understood the makeup of men. She was neither threatened nor intimidated by his frank confession. Because of this, they were able to protect their marriage commitment to one another.

Randy: Men of God who have studied and researched this whole issue of sight-stimulation say there isn't anything abnormal or sinful about a man noticing and thinking, "That woman is attractive" or "There's a good-looking girl over there." That isn't what's wrong. You get into trouble when you look, begin to undress her in your mind, and let your imagination (the devil's playground) go crazy.

You'll know when you've crossed the line because the Holy Spirit dwelling in you will deal with your spirit and warn you of danger. I feel the anointing of the Holy Ghost as I write these words to help you if you are struggling in this area. Perhaps you feel as though you're messing up in your moral behavior and endangering your marriage because of these thoughts going on in your mind.

Number one, recognize that God made you the way you are. The sensually-aware part of you is never going to change. That's why you must purpose to keep your body under subjection (self-discipline) *every* single day.

Number two, realize that men are born hunters. We see something and want to conquer it. Take shopping, for instance. When I go shopping for shoes, I decide ahead of time exactly which store I'm going to. I get out of my car, go in, look for the shoe rack, pick out the shoes, put them on the counter, pull out my credit card, pay for the shoes, *and I'm gone.* I've conquered the situation in a very short time.

Here's another illustration. Some men seem to have a distinctive attitude about travel. My Uncle Wayne will drive from Maryland to Tampa in twelve hours. Why? Because he likes the sense of conquering something. When he arrives, Uncle Wayne will say, "I drove here in twelve hours. I only went to the bathroom one time and that was in a cup." Women, on the other hand . . .

RECOGNIZE THAT GOD MADE YOU THE WAY YOU ARE. THE SENSUALLY-AWARE PART OF YOU IS NEVER GOING TO CHANGE.

Paula: I'll tell you about women! But first, here's a biological fact we need to know about men. Men favor the left side of their brain. They are logic-oriented because their brain is washed in testosterone while in the womb. This results in men becoming "lateral thinkers" who concentrate their thoughts on only one side of the brain at a time (switching between the analytical and the creative functions, respectively). So men are truly brain damaged. It's a scientific fact straight out of the medical books.

Female fetuses, however, do not experience this profusion of male hormones, and their brains remain intact. Their ability to think with both sides of their brain at the same time is greater than their male counterparts. Women tend to be a little more creative than men. And men who are creative tend to be somewhat feminine compared to other men.

Women see things clearer. We call it intuition. We see that woman coming after our man with her low-cut blouse, bringing him coffee a few too many times. And all the time our husbands are saying, "Nah, she doesn't like me. She is not after me, honey. No, she's not."

News flash! We women collect information like a computer. We store it until a signal goes off that says, "Uh-oh, uh-oh, uh-oh, wrong motive, wrong motive!" We process things that men don't process. That man doesn't see it until the other woman is standing buck naked in front of him. Then he says, "Hmm, maybe she *is* after me."

Randy: This actually happened to us a few years ago. Paula kept telling me, "Watch that girl. She's after you." I always replied, "Honey, she's not after me. She's just being nice. She wants to be mentored." I didn't have a clue.

Paula: As usual, because the left side of his brain has been washed in testosterone, he can't help it. It's a scientific, biological thing!

Randy: I'll never forget this. The woman was scheduled to come in at ten o'clock for a counseling session. But when I got to the office around 7:30 that Friday morning, she was already there! When I walked into my office, she just came right in, closed the door, and went into this seductive mode. I quickly called Paula and said, "Help! You're right. Get over here now!"

Paula: He actually sneaked out because he saw where she was headed. Then he started acting like a little boy, saying, "Come here right away. You're right—she's after me!" So mama handled it.

What makes women "different"?

Randy: Okay, we've talked about how men are sight-stimulated and have a strong sexual drive. They also seem to have a tendency for conquest. Women are not that way—they are different for sure.

Paula: Women are emotionally-stimulated. This is why you often see a beautiful woman with the most unattractive old man, and everyone's saying, "How did that guy get her?" That's easy. Because he wooed her and told her all the things she needed to hear. He made her feel good inside, all warm and secure. It's important to understand that a woman's emotions are not very stable. Women's emotions vary because of chemical fluctuations. We have periods, hormones, menopause, and everything else.

A smart man will start charting that time of the month for his woman and begin to understand that she cries for two days before she starts her period, thinks the whole world is coming to an end, that he doesn't love her anymore, and she's going to divorce court tomorrow. If you guys can hang on for just forty-eight hours, she's going to be okay.

That's when Pastor Randy should go out and buy me a new dress and tell me how much he loves me. Instead, he usually says, "I'm going to buy you a plane ticket. Don't you have someplace to go preach?"

SHE SAYS . . . HE SAYS

Here's another major difference between the sexes. Women are not only emotionally-stimulated, but we speak between 25,000 and 50,000 words a day. Men talk less than half that much—only 10,000-15,000 words a day. So this can be a major problem.

Randy: Let me interject an important note here that most men will relate to. You get up early, work all day long to provide an income for your family, and you're tired when you get home. You've dealt with a lot of junk all day—profanity, men cussing, telling dirty jokes around the office, or whatever. You're tired of the noise and the confusion of talking and being talked to. You can't wait for some peace and quiet.

But the minute you get home and walk in the door, your wife greets you with—"What did you do today? Who did you see and what did you talk about?" I don't know, maybe it's just me, but all I care to say is that I worked. What else am I supposed to say? "I had a great time. Let's move on. We're done right here." Now, if couples could figure out how to get past this daily confrontation, they could have a great victory.

I've discovered that Paula is not going to be happy if I say, "What do you think I was doing? I worked." I'm satisfied just to say, "I worked," but that isn't going to do it for her. It's absolutely not what she wants to hear.

After many years of marriage, I'm starting to learn some keys that help prepare me for that evening reunion. For example, I've found that it's a good idea to write down some of the highlights of my day to mention to her, because I know she's going to ask me about them. Now, it's not that she's interrogating me. She wants to be a part of what I'm involved in. I'm learning this.

Now, this is honestly what she wants to hear, "I got up this morning, brushed my teeth with Colgate toothpaste, took a shower, got dressed, and went to the garage, where I got into the car. I put the key in the ignition and shifted into reverse. Then I drove out. I got to the red light, turned left, and stopped at 7-Eleven. I put cream in the cup of coffee I bought there and added some Sweet 'n Low."

Paula: "And who did you talk to at 7-Eleven?"

Randy: "Yes, of course. I picked up a newspaper, paid for it and my coffee, and finally I got to work." Just look at the details she wants to know about before I even get to work! You thought it was just your wife who wanted to know. It's not just your wife—it is all women. Women are detail-oriented. They *love* details. God is teaching me this.

Men are headline-oriented. In other words, they don't have to read the entire newspaper to know what's going on—they can just look at the headlines. That's why it's kind of like that phrase we're always saying, "just give me the bottom line, please." Men want the facts—we don't need details.

Paula has learned that when I first come home, I need a little time alone. I believe lots of men are like this. Home is kind of like our cave. We want to be left alone for awhile. When we are ready to share and communicate, we'll come out.

Paula and I just recently had a big argument because I walked into our house and three church members were sitting in my living room who all wanted to hug me. I was thinking, *What are these people doing here? I don't want to hug anybody right now. I just want to go to the bedroom and pull the covers over my head.*

Later, of course, she wanted details as to why I was in such a bad mood.

Paula: I knew better, but I went with it anyway. My need to speak between 25,000 and 50,000 words a day was part of the reason. Talking so much can be a woman's greatest strength and greatest weakness. Women are better communicators than men. We learn to express our feelings better than men because we are communicators.

But notice that the Bible never calls a man a nag. You never see the Bible addressing a man about being idle, a gossip, or a busybody. We women use so many words (our greatest strength), but it becomes our greatest weakness when we are frustrated because we aren't aware of how to temper or control it. Our mouths just run.

And we run our mouths to the wrong people, at the wrong time, in the wrong places. So learn this lesson in life. Your husband needs his quiet time. When he's ready to talk, he'll talk to you.

Another thing I'm learning is that our need to talk often causes us to interrupt conversations when we don't feel that we are receiving enough details.

Randy: **Isn't this helpful? Now you're going to be able to relate and be encouraged because here's a pastor and his wife who are dealing with the very same issues you're dealing with. I often say, "Paula, you want the details. I'm telling you the details. Don't interrupt!"**

Paula: But he leaves out things I want to hear, and I can tell when there's more. If I keep on interrupting Randy—and I can tell by the look on his face when he's going to do this—he simply says, "I won't tell you anymore. You have to learn your lesson."

Then he clams up and no amount of apologizing will get him to continue telling me the juicy details. He puts me through acts of humility. Sometimes he makes me get on my knees and kiss his feet or something. One time he made me do a cartwheel in the mall. And I did it! I was desperate for communication!

Randy: Let's review the points we've covered so far. Man was birthed into productivity. Before he had a wife, he had responsibilities. That's why a man tends to view his worth based on what he does. When a man is going through something like changing jobs, he isn't programmed to be able to handle it well. He has temporarily lost his ability to be productive, and that makes him uncomfortable in his own skin. That's when the wise wife will cut him some slack. Don't nag him about it. This is an especially good time for the woman in his life to demonstrate her unequalled abilities to be charming and understanding.

Other points we've covered in this chapter—the woman is the help meet, birthed into relationship.

Men are sight-stimulated, hunters, and conquerors. They use 10,000 to 15,000 words a day.

Women are emotionally-stimulated. They need at least thirteen touches a day to feel secure. This is the truth. One of our associate pastors majored in psychology and counseling. He gave me a "Personality Profile" about five years ago that was amazingly accurate. You tell them, honey.

Paula: Everyone needs to do a "Personality Profile," which is the next point we're going to come to—understanding and identifying needs. Randy's profile said he could live on an island all by himself. He needs no communication, no affection . . . no anything. He is so self-sufficient that he doesn't need to receive anything from anybody. So he doesn't give out much either. He could be happy being a totally isolated person. It's the truth.

I have actually trained Randy to be affectionate because he didn't know how to show affection. But I had to learn to understand that this is normal for him—it is his makeup.

Randy: **Many men are like this. Typically, men are not "touchy-feely." We have to be trained. Men need to have the Holy Spirit do a work on them in the area of expressing affection. But let's talk more about these thirteen touches a woman needs every day.**

THE BASIC NEEDS OF MEN AND WOMEN IN MARRIAGE

Paula: This is important. When Randy and I were first married, he never touched me unless it was for sex. It made me feel like a piece of meat because I wanted to be touched, but not just when he wanted to make love. He didn't know this. I had to express it to him as a part of properly communicating and appropriately timing my communication.

He listened to me when I told him how scientific studies had proven that women need to be touched thirteen times a day to feel really loved and secure.

We started out our marriage in a double bed. Randy said, "I need a bigger bed," so we bought a king-size bed. Again he said,

"I need a bigger bed," so we got a European king-size bed. It is so big that you need a bullhorn to make anyone hear you from one side of this bed to the other.

Randy would be intimate with me during sexual intercourse, then roll all the way over to his European side and be a happy camper. I thought, *Forget that, buddy.* But I was learning and adjusting to the information I was getting on appreciating our differences, so I expressed my need for him to hold me during the night. Now he holds me. I need a lot of affection, and because I wake up anywhere from five to seven times during the night, I want to wake up being held. That communicates security to me.

Randy: **Good. Now let's talk about his needs/her needs. A man's needs differ greatly from those of a woman. In his book, *His Needs, Her Needs,* psychologist Dr. Willard F. Harley, Jr. identifies five basic needs men expect their wives to fulfill and five basic needs women expect their husbands to meet. In identifying these needs, Dr. Harley has helped thousands of couples improve their marriages.**

Although it is a given that each individual may have unique needs and preferences, there is a proven consistency about these two sets of five categories.

The five most basic needs in marriage tend to be:

For Men	For Women
1. Sexual fulfillment	1. Affection
2. Recreational companionship	2. Conversation
3. An attractive spouse	3. Honesty and openness
4. Domestic support	4. Financial support
5. Admiration	5. Family commitment

Although these categories may not apply equally to everyone, Dr. Harley's experience is that a majority of each sex agrees that these are their deepest needs in the marriage relationship.

No one should be surprised that *man's number-one marital need is sexual fulfillment.* God created sex, and He knew what He was doing. In fact, He designed sex to be pleasurable and thoroughly enjoyable. God made it all work and fit together for our pleasure.

Because of their background and past experiences, some people view sex differently. They feel that sex is wrong. But there is nothing wrong with it! Statistics indicate that men think about sex 70 percent of the time that they spend thinking.

Paula: My goodness, how are you all able to be so productive? I'm still learning. One time I asked, "Lord, why did You make men this way and leave us women the way we are?" I think it's because if we were both the same way, all we would do is chase each other all day, and we'd never accomplish anything at all.

Randy: Let me help you with this. Several years ago I counseled with one of the women of our church who felt that sex was dirty. She perceived sex as a duty she had to perform in order to make her husband feel better, but for her it was just something she wanted to have over with. She had never ever thought of sex as something beautiful created by God. Like Paula, this woman had been abused as a child. But she had sought no healing and had received none.

This is an issue because if men are not being fulfilled sexually in the bedroom by their spouse, they're going to want to go outside their bedroom. It's an issue that must be dealt with. This particular couple had been married for more than twenty years, lived in the same house, but slept in different bedrooms. This man was crying out, "I have sexual needs, and she's not meeting them!"

WHAT THE BIBLE SAYS ABOUT SEX

Paula: First Corinthians 7:3-5 AMP says, *The husband should give to his wife her conjugal rights (goodwill, kindness, and what is due her as his wife), and likewise the wife to her husband. For the wife does not have [exclusive] authority and control over her own body, but the husband [has his rights]; likewise also the husband does not have [exclusive] authority and control over his body, but the wife [has her rights]. Do not refuse and deprive and defraud each other [of your due marital rights], except perhaps by mutual consent for a time, so that you may devote yourselves unhindered to prayer. But afterwards resume marital relations, lest Satan tempt you [to sin] through your lack of restraint of sexual desire.*

Unfortunately, the teaching of this scripture passage makes some people very uncomfortable. Some even have a hard time believing that these verses are in *their* Bible. Well, take a look—they are in your Bible. I believe the enemy of our souls does his utmost to spread his lies throughout the body of Christ on this subject because he knows that when the two become one flesh, they are literally doing spiritual warfare when they make love. I, for one, firmly believe this to be true. Sex is a most holy union created by God—it's not dirty to Him. Read the Song of Solomon!

I've heard the Song of Solomon described as the Bible's *mystery* book. It is the only book in the Bible that seems to have been edited and censored by the Christian church. Most Christians don't read it, don't understand it, and have rarely, if ever, heard a sermon taken from it.

Read the Song of Solomon where the beloved kissed the breasts of his bride and further detailed one of the most romantic descriptions ever written of a sexual union. Her breasts alone are mentioned in this book eight or nine times!

Getting back to the scripture in 1 Corinthians 7, you are not to deny each other sexual pleasure unless the two of you have agreed to abstain from it for a prescribed period of time for some purpose *about which both of you agree.*

Now, there are some spooky, weird women out there who need to get at the root of why they have sexual hang-ups. I was sexually abused when I was a girl, and as a result, I had sexual hang-ups. I thought if a man gained access to my body, he would hurt and abuse it. It took a great deal of patience on Randy's part to work this out with me.

Men may have to work through some serious emotional baggage with women like me who have been hurt, abused, rejected, and abandoned. It took time for Randy to understand that I don't just give my body while we make love—I give my emotions, my whole being.

Randy can give me his body and be out of there, a happy camper. But I have to trust him with everything that is in me. A wife is vulnerable, so her husband needs to love her, emotionally stimulate her, and reaffirm her with his words and tenderness. He must lovingly and patiently work to develop and maintain a mutually fulfilling relationship with her.

I thank God that Randy was patient while God did a work of healing in my life. Now we have complete sexual freedom and fun in our bedroom.

Now, as I mentioned before, there are some weird, spooky women out there who choose to act all "spiritual" and start fasting when it's time to get intimate. You're not allowed to fast or pray unless you have permission from your husband, according to the Word of God. So there! You are required to take care of each other's sexual needs. So don't use those weird, spiritual guru routines to cover up your sexual hang-ups. Get to the root of the problem. Ask God to reveal what the problem is in your life. Once you get to the root of it, you can conquer it.

YOU'RE NOT ALLOWED TO FAST OR PRAY UNLESS YOU HAVE PERMISSION FROM YOUR HUSBAND, ACCORDING TO THE WORD OF GOD. SO THERE!

Randy: **There was a generation that just refused to deal with these issues, and they passed down their hang-ups to the next generation. They insisted that sex was dirty, improper, even sinful, but they couldn't have been more wrong. If this kind of misinformation was handed down to you, let it go. Get out from under it. It doesn't belong to you just because you "inherited" it from your parents. Deal with it, and set yourself free!**

WHAT ABOUT ORAL SEX?

Most of the things that people bring up in counseling with their spouse about sex and marriage involve what is and is not acceptable in the marriage bed—oral sex and masturbation are the most frequently mentioned.

Hebrews 13:4 says, *Marriage is honourable in all, and the bed undefiled: but whoremongers and adulterers God will judge.* I believe that God leaves much of our sexual relationship with our spouse to our discretion.

If two consenting, married adults who love each other agree on something, I believe it's okay.

Paula: Can we break this down even more? Please let me explain this because I want to help you. The Bible says the bed is undefiled. These two consenting adults Randy is talking about are two Christians. If both you and your spouse have the spirit of God, it's an impossibility for you to have a spirit of perversion.

Is it permissible to have oral sex? Most biblical scholars say the Scriptures are silent about oral-genital sex, which doesn't declare it to be right or wrong. Others say that the following verse in Song of Solomon refers to oral sex. Chapter 2, verse 3 says, *As the apple tree among the trees of the wood, so is my beloved among the sons. I sat down under his shadow with great delight, and his fruit was sweet to my taste.* A study of the word *fruit* shows that it refers to the male genitals throughout the Song of Solomon.

Some women may be horrified and repulsed by even talking about this. As we've said before, everyone is different. And please understand that Randy and I are not suggesting that you incorporate oral sex into your lovemaking activities. It is clearly a decision you need to make together privately. If it troubles you in any way, talk to God about it. Ask Him about every part of your sexual relationship. He came up with the idea of sex, and He is definitely a storehouse of wisdom on any subject you can possibly approach Him with.

Randy: Paula and I are in agreement on this topic with authors Linda Dillow and Lorraine Pintus, both of whom are involved in Christian ministry. In their practical, biblically based book, *Intimate Issues: 21 Questions Christian Women Ask About Sex,* there are ten things that God specifically forbids people to participate in at all: fornication, adultery, homosexuality, impurity, orgies, prostitution, lustful passions, sodomy, obscenity and coarse jesting (filthy jokes), and incest.

If you don't believe these things are issues with *real* Christians, you are mistaken. Christians are struggling with lust because of sexual issues the church hasn't addressed. It is the church's responsibility to teach people what the Word of God has to say about sexual issues. Too many preachers have danced around the subject by saying things like there's only one acceptable sexual position (missionary). These same preachers have been caught with prostitutes! What's wrong with this picture?

Also, if your parents weren't able to engage in frank discussions with you on the subject because of their timidity, embarrassment, or even shame, you're somewhat handicapped from a practical perspective. Pray and ask God what is best for you. He will let you know His feelings on the subject as it relates to you personally.

IS YOUR SPOUSE YOUR BEST FRIEND?

Now let's look at the *man's number-two need—recreational companionship.*

Paula: Your husband needs you to be his friend. Remember all the things you did with him when you were dating? You loved it when he worked out and got all sweaty. That was so sexy to you. You'd go with him to football games and boxing matches because you loved him and wanted to impress him with your undivided attention and interest in what interested him.

> CHRISTIANS ARE STRUGGLING WITH LUST BECAUSE OF SEXUAL ISSUES THE CHURCH HASN'T ADDRESSED.

But the moment you said, "I do" and he came home from the gym sweating, you said, "Oh, yuck . . . go take a shower!" All of a sudden, football no longer held your interest. You saw it as a bunch of dirty, overgrown, fat men throwing a pigskin. And you'd rather be at the mall.

Your husband needs recreational companionship. One of the reasons he fell in love with you was because you took an interest in what he was interested in, including his yucky, sweaty body and all those overgrown men throwing a pigskin across a chalk line.

Randy: **Amen. *Man's number-three need is an attractive spouse.* This gets back to the man being sight-stimulated. If you don't believe that, read 1 Samuel 16:7. It says man looks** on the outward appearance, but God looks on the heart. Man judges people by the way he sees things. That's why it's important for women to understand—even if you've been married for fifteen to twenty years or more—that men like for their wives to keep themselves looking nice.

Paula has always dressed nicely. Her hair is always done. She usually has on makeup. She is very attractive, and I like to come home to her. That's my preference.

I have been greeted at their front doors by women from my church (who knew I was coming over) with curlers in their hair, wearing a ragged bathrobe they'd had the entire forty-five years they'd been married, and big, old, ugly bedroom slippers—at five o'clock in the afternoon! They'd been laying on the couch, eating Reese's Peanut Butter Cups and watching soap operas!

When their husbands come home from work, they have to fix their own dinner!

Let me tell you something important right here. Your man won't go window-shopping anywhere else if he has a Rolls Royce sitting in his driveway. Do you get my drift?

Women always need to keep in mind that men are sight-stimulated. You don't have to look like Pamela Anderson. All you need to do is fix yourself up. Take a bath, brush your teeth, gargle with some pleasant-tasting mouthwash. Put on some makeup, a nice outfit, and spray on some perfume. Fix him a candlelight dinner.

Never forget, there's a Delilah out there, and her eyes are on your Samson.

Finally, be thankful for what you have. I thank God every day for my wife. She carries a load that makes my life easier. She makes me shine.

Let's not let men off the hook. No! Some men can be selfish and self-centered, but they need to make their wives shine. Take your wife out to a restaurant once in awhile. Get a babysitter. Plan an evening out.

You may have looked like Robert Redford when you first got married, but now you look like Kojak. I don't know what it is about age, but it does funny things to you. Guys get these big rubber tubes around their mid-section.

Paula: All these things are important. You know, Randy, the Bible says a woman is her man's glory (see 1 Corinthians 11:7). In many European and Middle Eastern cultures, a woman who is well-groomed and attractive serves as an indicator that her husband is very successful. When people say, "Paula, you look nice," it's a compliment to Randy that he takes good care of me.

THE BLESSINGS OF PARTNERSHIP

Randy: *Domestic support is man's fourth most important need in marriage.* What does this mean? It's sort of an unspoken trade-off between most husbands and wives. He goes into the marriage believing she will be the cook, laundress, housekeeper, and caregiver of any children they will produce.

If the dishwasher goes on the blink, she will usually be the one who calls the repairman.

Husbands feel they are meeting their responsibilities in providing the income the family needs and enjoys. It is true that most women today work outside the home and contribute income to the household. With the "liberation" of women, we've pretty much left the Cleavers and the Nelsons of fifty years ago behind. But, to a large extent, working women are busier than they've ever been because the typical husband still needs the domestic tasks cared for in the way we have just described.

Men's and women's deep, basic needs have changed very little, and career women still find themselves coming home and doing much of the domestic things housewives have been doing for centuries.

Couples need to help each other carry the load. Since I can remember, my dad has done the grocery shopping every Saturday morning because my mother has always worked outside the home. Dad takes that shopping cart every week, fights the crowd of housewives and career women who don't have any time to shop for groceries except on Saturdays, and he takes care of the grocery shopping.

Beyond that, he vacuums the floors, cleans the bathrooms, and washes the dishes. My working parents work together as a team, but I believe Dad goes out of his way to do his part. It takes a man's man to do that, and I admire him. I'm getting convicted right now just writing about what a great husband my dad is and has been to my mom.

God wants us to share responsibilities equally. You do your part, and your spouse will do his or hers.

Finally, *a man needs to be admired.* It is a fact that a man is inspired to achievement when a woman lavishes her encouragement and attention on him. He begins to see himself as capable, efficient, and prepared both mentally and physically. He is more confident and certain about himself.

Not only does admiration motivate a man, it can be a satisfying reward for his accomplishments. A wife's admiration for her husband can be as fulfilling to him as his paycheck. Admiration is energizing because he can actually sense her tangible support.

BASIC NEEDS OF WOMEN IN MARRIAGE

Paula: *Women need affection—it is priority one on her list of things a woman most needs from her marriage.* Affection means "partiality, tender attachment, love, prejudice, propensity, disposition, warm regard." Affection implies approval and comfort, security and protection to a woman. The husband who demonstrates affection for his wife is saying, "I'm happy to be your protector and caregiver because no one is more important to me than you."

Husbands must clearly understand how strongly wives feel about affection. A simple hug can communicate all of the definitions of affection. Generally, women are huggers. They hug each other, children (anybody's), parents, siblings, aunts, uncles, cousins, members of their prayer group, their pastor, his or her spouse, and the lovely lady down at the retirement center who reminds them of Aunt Lucy.

I like to receive cards and flowers. Randy wasn't much of a card and flower sender, so I talked to his Supervisor, God. Now I receive flowers from time to time. Affection is essential to most women, and, as I've said before, it is very important to me. I had to teach Randy to be affectionate, but he's a fast learner. It is not nearly the issue in our marriage that it once was.

Randy: *Conversation is a woman's second most important factor in feeling secure about her marriage.* We've discussed it at some length already. Women have a need to release 25,000 to 50,000 words a day, but more importantly, they want their husbands to talk too.

Men have little trouble talking when they are dating. When Paula and I first met, she was going through the pain of a divorce. We liked each other and had pleasant discussions together. We had things in common—I'd been deeply hurt as a result of my own divorce, and both of us were desperately trying to hear from God and find a way to rebuild our lives.

I don't remember having difficulty relating all the details she is so eager to hear.

Statistically, three areas where marriages most often fail are sex, money, and communication. Most of the time, the weakness is communication . . . about sex and money. Once you get communication down, sex and money will usually follow. The husband who seriously desires to meet his wife's need for closeness will devote time and attention to being a good communicator.

Since we've already learned that a man's greatest need is sexual fulfillment and a wife's greatest need is affection, it easily follows that communication is an important factor in both of those. What better way to meet your partner's need for sex or affection than verbal communication and body language? Couples who openly communicate their desires and needs are happier and more compatible than those who don't.

Sharing information leads to a better understanding of what's going on in your mate's world. A husband needs to know when his wife thinks he's doing something right as much as he needs to know about anything he said or did that affected her negatively.

A WIFE'S SECRET WEAPON

Paula: When Randy didn't talk to me as much as I wanted him to, I got on my knees and said, "Lord, I am frustrated with this man. You've got to help me out here. I need some caressing down here. I need some flowers. I need some trips to the mall. I need him to just sit with me and hug me without it being a sexual thing. I want this man to hold my hand for a while and talk to me eye to eye for a minute or two. He just doesn't understand what I need." Then I kept my mouth shut. Prayer was my secret weapon.

I didn't go back and nag Randy about being more talkative and communicative. The next thing I knew, I started getting flowers. I came home one day, and there were candles out. There was a bubble bath ready and waiting for me. I said, "Dear God, I'm going to hit my knees more often."

Don't nag your husband about things. Just go to his Superior in your prayer closet and see what God can do to that man. You can't change him anyway.

The third basic need of women in marriage is for their husbands to be open and honest with them. I believe most people agree that honesty in a marriage is key to its success. Dishonesty in any relationship causes confusion, instability, and a state of disorder. We women have to be able to trust in order to give ourselves completely to a man.

Honesty works the other way too. When wives lie and tell their husbands that their new dress cost $80 when it was really $100, they'll lie about anything. Trust is built over a period of time. However, trust can be broken with one lie. Truth always prevents disaster.

We find that *financial support is the number-four slot out of the five most basic needs of a woman.* Do women marry for money? Yes! At least she expects her man to earn enough money to support her well. Some statistics say a woman wants to be supported at least as well as her father supported her when she was growing up—if not better than that.

Because my father committed suicide when I was five years old, our family's economic status was immediately and dramatically altered. My father had come from a family with money. After his death, my dad's family took over the family business, leaving no position for my mother. She was forced to seek other employment. She worked long, hard hours. I didn't really see her much.

When Randy met me, I was living in a trailer, growing my own groceries. I was so poor that I couldn't afford to pay attention. I was really messed up.

After we were married, Randy and I were making a lot of money up in Washington, D.C. when God called us to Tampa. We didn't know I was going to go without a paycheck for two years after the move. I didn't know when I married Randy that I'd have to sleep on a pee-stained mattress for awhile.

But I knew my God. He has never seen the righteous forsaken nor His seed begging for bread (see Psalm 37:25). I wasn't consumed with worry about finances because I believed that God would supply all of our needs according to His riches in glory (see

Philippians 4:19). I was confident that we were in the will of God.

If you thought it would be roses all the way when you got married, honey, I have a word for you. Trouble is no respecter of persons. It knocks on everybody's door sooner or later. You'd better have something strong on the inside of you to weather life's storms.

Yes, women need financial support. God's Word says that when a man doesn't provide for his family, he's worse than an unbeliever (see 1 Timothy 5:8). The consequences of a man not providing for his family will result in the woman taking control because she feels she has to make something happen. That will lead to chaos because God's plan for the family will be out of order.

WHY I MARRIED RANDY WHITE

Number five of the five most basic needs of women is security and family commitment. A woman needs to know that her husband is committed to her, their children, and to everything she deems important.

Randy is about nine and a half years older than me—I tease him about being an old man—but I needed that maturity in my life. I needed that stability. I was very young and had a great call and destiny on my life. Randy came to me and said,

TROUBLE IS NO RESPECTER OF PERSONS. IT KNOCKS ON EVERYBODY'S DOOR SOONER OR LATER.

"You're going to be my wife." It scared me. Why? I'd made mistakes. I'd had bad relationships, and I didn't want to make more.

It shook me because I did not have the confidence to believe I could hear the voice of God. It shook me so that I initially ran from the relationship because my way of dealing with things was—*I'll push you out before you get a chance to push me out. I'll abandon you before you abandon me.* There was a lot of baggage from my past.

Randy was very confident, but we didn't get married right away. The reason I married him, though, was not because of where we were or where we'd been, but what I knew. It wasn't about looks because, believe me, we both looked a whole lot different than we look now. I've got the pictures to prove it. He was about seventy pounds heavier. I was about forty pounds heavier. I dressed okay then, but he wore pink polyester suits, green velvet bow ties, and blue platform shoes! He had a little bowl haircut, but I knew a good barber.

Now women look at him and want him. I tell them to go get their own man and make him a husband. I had to find my own man. Isn't that what the Bible tells us? Train up a husband in the way he should go and when he's older, he'll not depart from it? Just kidding!

I married Randy because I knew we both wanted to be at the same place at the end of our lives. We had common goals to unite our destiny. Honest to goodness, you don't know if you're always going to be in love. I didn't know when I married him if he'd always make my eyes sparkle or make my toes tap or make my hands sweat.

My point is that if you can fall in love, you can also fall out of love. I didn't know when I married Randy how we would relate sexually or emotionally. I didn't know if it was all there. But I knew that I loved God, and I knew that Randy did too. And I knew we'd figure out everything in between. I figured if we had the same destination, we'd find a way to get there together. So we hooked up, and the rest is history.

HIS NEEDS/HER NEEDS:
APPRECIATING THE DIFFERENCES

1. **Man was birthed into productivity.**
   a. Had a job before he had a wife
   b. Is stimulated by sight, not emotions
   c. Prefers headlines to details
   d. Uses between 10,000 and 15,000 words a day
   e. Enjoys quality time alone

2. **Woman was born into relationship.**
   a. Was a wife before she had a job
   b. Is stimulated by emotions, not sight
   c. Prefers details to headlines
   d. Needs to use 25,000 to 50,000 words a day;
      needs thirteen touches daily
   e. Enjoys feeling secure

3. **Marriages are meant to complete—not compete.**

4. **The five basic needs in marriage...**
   a. For Men:
      1. Sexual fulfillment
      2. Recreational companionship
      3. An attractive spouse
      4. Domestic support
      5. Admiration
   b. For Women:
      1. Affection
      2. Conversation
      3. Honesty and openness
      4. Financial support
      5. Family commitment

5. **Sex: What is acceptable in the Christian bed?**

6. **Sharing responsibilities in the home.**

HOMEWORK ASSIGNMENT

Husbands

1. Discover something you can do to make your wife feel secure about your relationship.
2. Practice giving her the thirteen tender but not sexual touches she needs each day.
3. Set aside a period of time this week to give your wife your undivided attention. Listen to all her details without appearing to be bored, and share something with her that happened to you at work this week.

Wives

1. Try motivating your husband through his ego. Find something you can compliment him about.
2. Before he gets home from work, take a long, hot bubble bath, fix your hair, and apply makeup. Put on something especially attractive, and flirt!
3. Light some candles in your bedroom. Leave a love note on his pillow.

Father, I appreciate the insights on relationships shared in this chapter. I believe that I am in the process of gaining much wisdom and knowledge from reading this book. I believe my attitudes and thoughts are changing for the better. Strengthen me, Lord, that I may be a godly example in everything I do. Help me to be full of love for others, following Christ's example, who loves me and gave Himself as a sacrifice that I might enjoy life in abundance (including my marriage)! Thank You for giving me understanding about the differences in men and women. I ask You to give me the right words to effectively communicate with my spouse. I praise You for Your grace and blessing on my spouse, my marriage, and my family. Amen.

two

MARRIAGE CAN'T WORK WITHOUT GOD

Randy: A great marriage doesn't just *happen.* Think about it—two imperfect people, with all their flaws and frailties, are drawn together largely by physical and character attraction, and the church, along with the world, suggests they get married and "make it work!" How can two such imperfect vessels combine to establish a perfect union?

We are convinced that marriage absolutely cannot work unless both the husband and the wife are willing and able to put God first—before one another and before the two families that produced them.

A marriage without faith in God doesn't stand a chance in the crazy, anything goes, situation ethics, do-whatever-pleases-you, instant gratification, all-you-can-eat, drive-through world where we live. Why? Because just the act of agreeing that God has first place in every aspect of the marriage declares that the two of you are starting out on common ground. That, in itself, is an achievement! And there's power in agreement, according to the Word of God.

You can't get away from it—faith in God has to come first. You can't even build your relationship, much less your future together, without faith. It is the divine order of things.

Paula and I have developed what we call the six "Fs" as key issues in our relationship. They are not a formula for a successful marriage, because only the Bible provides the foolproof formula, but they are important to the success of most, if not all, relationships:

1. Faith
2. Fitness
3. Family
4. Finances
5. Fellowship
6. Fun

You can't get away from it—faith in God has to come first.

In this chapter, we're going to talk about each of these "Fs," and you can put them in whatever order you feel they'll work best for you, but number one still has to be faith. In order to obtain God's promises, you have to operate in God's principles. Let's take a look at some examples.

Wives, submit yourselves unto your own husbands, as unto the Lord. For the husband is the head of the wife, even as Christ is the head of the church: and he is the saviour of the body. Therefore as the church is subject unto Christ, so let the wives be to their own husbands in every thing.

—Ephesians 5:22-24

Paula: Although we will address the issue of submission in depth later, I want to offer some practical applications to what we've already said. Even the word *submit* was like a curse word to me when Randy and I were first married—especially since he has such a strong personality. I used to pray, "God, help Randy. All the problems in our marriage are his fault. Please do something! He needs to be more Casanova-like. He needs to be romantic and send me flowers.

"Let him just woo me and love me like You love the church. Help him to understand me. Let him know what it's like to have PMS. God, do something with this man. He doesn't even notice that I've lost weight or changed my hair color from red to brown to blonde all in one week!"

My prayer may sound silly to you, but I was sincere in asking for the Lord's help. Imagine my surprise when God said, "I can't." Now, I really had a problem with that. I thought, *Why can't You help him? You're God! Surely You can do something with my problem here.* But God said, "I can't help Randy because I've told you to submit, and you have not."

One meaning of the word *submit* is "to duck." I had to learn to "duck" and get out of the way so God could make Randy the husband I wanted and desired. It's a godly principle that works. The moment I got out of His way, God had the ability to get to Randy White. And guess what? It wasn't long before I started receiving flowers. I began to be wooed (was he flirting with me?). He started looking at me with a twinkle in his eye. I thought we were on our honeymoon again . . . after many, many years.

That's why we learned to put God first. We now base our marriage *completely* on the Word of God. Before, we *said* it was based on the Word, but we were wearing masks to cover up what was really going on. You must understand this: I don't submit because Randy tells me to. I do it because the Word of God asks me to. And we both understand that there are boundaries.

It is very important for you to realize that the principles we're talking about apply to two people who are loving and serving God. We are not talking about a believer and an unbeliever or even two unbelievers. Our focus here is on Christian marriages. God never asks anyone to submit to sin. If your spouse is not a Christian and asks you to do something contrary to the Word of God, you are under no obligation to submit to his requests. We'll deal with that later in the book.

Randy: I love, honor, cherish, and adore my wife, but there are times when she's just plain unlovable. How do I live with Paula when she's unlovable? How do I love her when she's nagging me and grating on my very last nerve? For us, it's time to get away—to put a little distance between us.

Paula is regularly invited to speak at churches and women's conferences all over the country. These brief separations work very well for us. From time to time, I laughingly tell her, "I'm buying you a plane ticket and sending you off to preach somewhere. I'll see you next week when I get the victory over you!"

This scenario may work well for Randy and Paula White, but we realize it wouldn't work for everyone. More important to the point in this portion of our study is how does a woman who has never seen godly submission in action submit to her husband? If a woman has never witnessed her mother or grandmother submitting to her husband—perhaps because her father or grandfather never assumed his rightful role—how does she go about developing that quality in herself? Again, it's through the principle of putting God first or submitting herself to the Lord.

SUBMISSION? HOW DOES IT WORK?

The way we do many things is a direct result of how we are taught. Of course, the best way to learn anything is by example, and if you didn't have a good example to follow while you were growing up, it will be much more difficult to know exactly how to do whatever it is you're attempting to learn. Parents should be our first teachers, but, sadly, they are often examples of what not to do—how not to behave.

Paula: The truth is that many women don't know how to submit because the church has not been a good model of being subject to Christ as it should be. This is the key. In all honesty, it isn't difficult for me to submit to Randy now because Randy loves me as Christ loves the church. But if a husband hasn't assumed his rightful role as priest of his household, his wife feels insecure and lacks trust in her husband. *Will he hurt me? Is he going to abandon me? Could he become abusive if I don't meet his demands and expectations?*

Submission is made much easier for the Christian wife of a Christian husband because of God's instructions found in Ephesians 5:25-30 AMP:

> *Husbands, love your wives, as Christ loved the*
> *church and gave Himself up for her, so that He might*

sanctify her, having cleansed her by the washing of water with the Word, that He might present the church to Himself in glorious splendor, without spot or wrinkle or any such things [that she might be holy and faultless]. Even so husbands should love their wives as [being in a sense] their own bodies. He who loves his own wife loves himself. For no man ever hated his own flesh, but nourishes and carefully protects and cherishes it, as Christ does the church, because we are members (parts) of His body.

Randy: Faith in God alone is the foundation of every successful marriage. It sounds simplistic, but a married couple must be free to pray together, share the Word of God together, and be intimate with one another concerning God's Word. This command in Ephesians 5 is directed toward a husband to love his wife so much that he wants to do everything he can to make her happy. No wife will have trouble with the submission issue when her husband is doing what the Word of God has directed him to do. This isn't as difficult an issue as people—and even the church—have made it appear.

I love to give to Paula because when she's happy, I'm happy. If she's not happy, I don't stand a chance. First Corinthians 11:7 AMP says that she is my glory: . . . *woman is [the expression of] man's glory (majesty, preeminence).*

When a wife wants to have her nails done, her husband needs to just give her the money and let her go and get her nails done. He doesn't need to fuss and complain about things like that. Husbands, your wife's efforts to look her best reflect on you. It says you care enough to give her the very best that you have. Your generosity makes her feel honored and cherished. That's how God cares for you, and this is how He expects you to care for your wife.

Women are not made like men. Ephesians 5:29-31 says, *For no man ever hated his own flesh, but nourishes and carefully protects and cherishes it, as Christ does the church, because we are members (parts) of His body. For this reason a man shall leave his father and his mother and shall be joined to his wife, and the two shall become one flesh.* Thank God for His Word!

> WHEN A WIFE WANTS TO HAVE HER NAILS DONE, HER HUSBAND NEEDS TO JUST GIVE HER THE MONEY AND LET HER GO AND GET HER NAILS DONE.

God first. If He is not number one in your marriage, your marriage is out of order. I know there are preachers, marriage counselors, and seminars that tell you they have a certain formula that *always* works. But I'm telling you, I don't believe them, and this is why: everybody is different. Our lifestyles are different, and we have to do what works for us.

We've seen couples come back from a highly-touted marriage seminar in a worse mess than when they went. They've tried to put themselves in the box that was suggested to them as the foolproof way to a successful marriage and attempted to conform to something that simply doesn't fit them and their situation. What works for one couple probably won't work exactly the same way for another. Just because it works for the seminar speaker and his or her spouse doesn't mean it will work for you.

Paula: Allow me to use my travel schedule as an example of what works well for Randy and me. If I stayed home all the time—even though that is not my assignment—I would kill Randy or he would kill me. One of us would be dead, and the other one would be in prison by now because we would be out of the will of God. Being out of God's will produces frustration . . . and frustration leads to all manner of ungodly behavior.

For us, it's healthy for me to be gone two or three days a week. Randy and I feel peace about it. It works for us.

Randy: I've been in church all my life. I've been in the ministry for more than twenty-five years myself. There is a reason why more than 50 percent of all marriages end in divorce—including Christian marriages. There is a reason why 60 percent of all spouses are having extramarital affairs—statistics say that six of ten couples who are having extramarital affairs attend church regularly. Is that unbelievable or what? Sadly, it's true.

Why? It's largely true because the church has refused to deal with the hard-core issues. We've got to get real. It's time to take off the masks we wear to impress other people and get down to the nitty-gritty.

It's time we stopped going to the psychologist, the psychotherapist, and the Oprah Winfrey Show to find out what they have to say about marriage and the family. It's time to get back to the Word of God because He has ordained and instituted marriage. He has given us an A-to-Z plan to tell us how to make it work.

WE'VE GOT TO GET REAL. IT'S TIME TO TAKE OFF THE MASKS WE WEAR TO IMPRESS OTHER PEOPLE AND GET DOWN TO THE NITTY-GRITTY.

Marriage is a divine institution ordained by almighty God. Marriage is God's will.

THE KLEENEX MENTALITY

We live in a throwaway society. I sometimes call it a "Kleenex mentality"—if it's messed up, throw it away. That disposable attitude extends into human relations as well. Marriage not working? Junk it. Pregnancy inconvenient? Abort it. Kids causing trouble? Throw them out, send them to live with grandparents, or look into boarding schools. Friends becoming a drag? It's your way or the highway—say "so long" and move on.

Paula: The church at large hasn't dealt with these important issues. The church needs some cleaning up. God began a clean-up program in the pulpits a few years ago that is just now beginning to have a positive effect. It isn't that the church is corrupt—it has just avoided dealing with touchy, uncomfortable issues, and our marriages and families have paid the price.

FITNESS

Know ye not that ye are the temple of God, and that the Spirit of God dwelleth in you? If any man defile the temple of God, him shall God destroy; for the temple of God is holy, which temple ye are.

—1 CORINTHIANS 3:16,17

Randy: While these verses are not just talking about going to the gym and working out, we will discuss the importance of keeping our physical bodies in good condition. But in this case, we're talking about taking care of ourselves—body, soul, and spirit—so we can care for each other.

The relationship we have with our family illustrates our relationship with God. First John 4:20 says, *If a man say, I love God, and hateth his brother, he is a liar: for he that loveth not his brother whom he hath seen, how can he love God whom he hath not seen?*

When priorities are wrong, weakness and failures are imminent. How we prioritize our lives—the order of importance in which we place things—is key to any successful relationship, but it is especially critical to the marriage relationship.

Paula: *Priority Number 1: You cannot love yourself until you have received God's love.* Once you know how much God loves you, then you can love yourself and others. Do you see the order here? Receive God's love first, then love yourself, and last, love others.

Here's the problem between men and women. Men often marry women who are a certain size and body type because men are sight-stimulated. Men are hunters. They prowl around until they find a beautiful, shapely woman who has a voluptuous body in all the right places, with great legs, a mane of fabulous hair, gorgeous eyes, etc., etc. A year or so into the marriage, she gains fifty pounds or more—*not* in all the right places.

I know what I'm talking about because I gained 87 pounds while I was carrying my son. I know what it is to weigh more than 200 pounds, and I know what it is to be a normal size. I've had experience in this area.

This weight gain can cause problems in the relationship because the man has married someone who came in a much different package than the one he's looking at now. This is not the person he married. He had certain expectations of that person— a level of respect and admiration.

It's the same with men. Many women are attracted to a man who looks a certain way, and then he gets a beer gut on him that's hanging out everywhere, and he no longer remotely resembles the groom on top of the cake.

Randy: There are things we can do to maintain the package— to keep the package as attractive as it was during the hunt. I don't want to offend anyone, but I'm going to speak plainly about this. Do you think it's easy for me, as busy as my schedule is, to work out every day? It kills me. It takes total discipline to do it. I hate to get on that stairmaster. I hate to walk on the treadmill. I'd much rather have a pepperoni pizza smothered in cheese than to have a chicken sandwich or steamed vegetables.

But I love the results. I feel good about myself when my doctor takes a blood sample and says, "Your cholesterol and triglycerides are better than they've ever been." The workout is worth it to me.

ABUSING THE TEMPLE OF GOD—OUR BODIES

I believe this is one of the issues the church has overlooked for years and years. We have people in our prayer lines with sugar diabetes and all kinds of diseases. Why? People constantly are filling their stomachs full of junk, and it's time the body of Christ wakes up to these issues. *We really are what we eat!*

I read an interesting item in *Time* magazine recently. The president of one of the more prosperous African nations said, "My people are killing themselves with their forks!" He said the people are not only overweight, but their health is also deteriorating with diabetes, high cholesterol, and other conditions that lead to heart disease and cancer. If that's happening in Africa now, imagine how long it has been going on in America, even in the church. Even some of the TV preachers we see every week are obese. They're pacing across the platform out of breath and sweating, pulling out their big handkerchiefs and wiping their brows. Two or three chins hang over their tight collars, and you wonder if they'll have a heart attack right on the air. They have lost sight of their priorities. Something is definitely out of balance.

All of us need to take care of ourselves on the inside as well as on the outside. We need to learn about good nutrition, watch what and how much we eat, get adequate amounts of rest, take natural supplements that enhance a healthy lifestyle, and drink lots of water. These are just practical, common sense steps that anyone can take to become fit, look good, and feel great!

Paula: Let me interject something here from a wife's viewpoint. It makes me feel good that Randy takes care of himself because I want him to grow old with me. I don't want to lose him when he's forty-five or fifty years old. When I know his heart is good and his triglycerides are right, it says to me that he's going to live long. I'm not going to have to worry about growing old alone. It produces what I'm looking for (and all women have this basic need), which is emotional security. It's not about big, muscular biceps. I want Randy to be taking good care of me when he is ninety years old!

Randy: People don't like to talk about health and fitness— especially in the church—and this might make you angry at me right now, but we're going to go on. This is an issue whether you think so or not.

In the church, we'll tell you in a heartbeat not to curse, drink, smoke, chew, or sleep around. But gluttony is as much a sin as fornication. We do not take care of the temple of God. First Corinthians 3:16 AMP says, *Do you not discern and understand that you [the whole church at Corinth] are God's temple (His sanctuary), and that God's Spirit has His permanent dwelling in you [to be at home in you, collectively as a church and also individually]?*

You and I have a gift on the inside of us. *But we have this treasure in earthen vessels, that the excellency of the power may be of God, and not of us* (2 Corinthians 4:7). Compared to my spirit and my soul, my body is probably the least significant, but it has some significance. Many of the health problems we face are brought on by poor nutrition and a lack of discipline.

This may not be something you want to acknowledge, but your spiritual walk also comes down to discipline. The bottom line is this: are you crucifying your flesh so the Spirit of God can rule and reign in your life? How can you be spiritually disciplined if you can't discipline yourself physically?

Please don't misunderstand me. I realize that everyone is different. Fitness is relative to your individual needs and desires, bone structure, height, etc. Always consult a reputable physician before making a dramatic lifestyle change. Be led by God's peace and exercise wisdom.

Paula: Under the heading of fitness also comes being spiritually fit. First Timothy 4:8-10 AMP reminds us, *For physical training is of some value (useful for a little), but godliness (spiritual training) is useful and of value in everything and in every way, for it holds promise for the present life and also for the life which is to come. This saying is reliable and worthy of complete acceptance by everybody. With a view to this we toil and strive, [yes and] suffer reproach, because we have [fixed our] hope on the living God, Who is the Savior (Preserver, Maintainer, Deliverer) of all men, especially of those who believe (trust in, rely on, and adhere to Him).*

The context in which we are using the word *fitness* means taking care of yourself, because you cannot love others until you love yourself. And how can you give to your spouse and family if you can't take care of yourself?

You cannot give what you don't possess. So we're saying God comes first and then yourself. That may sound selfish, but if you are not whole, you cannot be an effective vessel fit for the Master's use. So when we talk about being fit, we're talking about caring for ourselves—spirit, soul, and body.

FAMILY

There was a great attack on the African-American household in the '60s. The target was the male head of the home, and this attack resulted in two-thirds of all African American families growing up without a father in the house. Fathers became an endangered species. In the '80s, the attack spread to Caucasian men. Dads no longer reside in about half of all of America's homes.

As a result of Satan's aggression against the family, husbands throughout this country and within the church have abandoned their wives (or never married them at all) and run from their responsibilities. God ordained the family and it is at the core of His perfect will for all Christians.

At the head of this family is Christ, then the husband, next his wife, and last, their children. This is God's rank of authority. *But I want you to know and realize that Christ is the Head of every man, the head of a woman is her husband, and the Head of Christ is God* (1 Corinthians 11:3 AMP). This might ruffle a few feathers for some women, but it is God's order for the household. As part of that order, we find that the man is accountable to God.

You see, God looks at us individually in terms of our relationship with Him. We have our own individual salvation. I can't get to heaven on Randy's coattail. I can't obtain blessings because I'm his wife. I do fall under an umbrella of favor, however, when it comes to the family unit. Although I have my own individual walk with God, when it comes to the family unit, God sees Randy and me as one.

But God holds Randy White—not me—accountable for how our household is run. This includes how we manage our finances and how our children are raised. The man has a great deal of responsibility, but God doesn't let women off the hook. He brought us along as helpers for these men, and there are things we can do that are more helpful if we do them God's way than if we insist on having our own way.

What does it mean to be *OBEDIENT?*

We've spoken briefly on submission, and we're going to go into it in chapter three with all the intensity that word consistently seems to generate. But wives also need to be obedient. Obedience to a husband in all things is based upon him loving his wife as Christ loves the church. Our submission and obedience as wives is based upon knowing that our husbands are required to be Christlike.

Would Christ talk to you like a dog? Would Christ sit in an overstuffed chair, drinking beer, watching football on TV for hours and hours, demanding that you fetch him sandwiches, chips, and a cushion for his feet? I don't think so. So obedience is not something you're obligated to perform if the man is not loving you as Christ loves the church.

Let me clarify this for some of you who were about to walk over to your husband and show him this page of the book—you can't expect your husband to walk around on tulips and tiptoes, going to the mall at the drop of your hat, taking you to see a romantic movie when his favorite team is playing in the Super Bowl, or cleaning out the garage right now because your mother is coming to visit.

That's manipulation, and it's a sin. I know because I was a world-class manipulator when Randy and I got together.

We were engaged and very serious, but I had a real problem with manipulation. I would venture to say that you probably did too until you got sanctified by the Holy Ghost. We women can manipulate things very well. We bat our eyes until we get men to eat out of our hands. I advise you both to watch out for that. It's a creepy little monster.

My father committed suicide when I was five years old, and I used that as an excuse for lots of different things. I'd cry and say, "You just don't know what it's like to be abandoned. . . ." One day Randy didn't respond to something I said as I'd expected him to, and that little demon came out in me. I just started bawling and squalling like a child.

Everybody else would just melt when I pulled a stunt like this and say, "Oh, poor baby . . . ," but Randy looked me squarely in the eye and said, "When you want to grow up and act like an adult, then we'll talk." Then he left. I cried louder and louder. It didn't work. About two hours later, I was mad. "I can't believe him! What a jerk!" I thought sure he'd come back.

The next day . . . no Randy White. Day two . . . no Randy White. Three weeks later . . . let me tell you, God dealt with me. I got rid of that manipulation demon. I got sanctified and set free from that thing. I had to sit on my bed and struggle with that because I didn't want to let it go. It got me things I didn't know how to get any other way.

If that manipulative demon has attached itself to you, let it go or it will wreck every single relationship you have or ever will have. It will ruin a family.

I had to release it to Jesus Christ myself—nobody else could do it for me. I dealt with that thing and, as I did, I really began to miss Randy. He's so stubborn, and I knew he wouldn't call me.

I figured he was probably dating someone else by then and had hocked my ring. So I called him.

He said, "Oh, I see you want to act like an adult now."

I didn't like it, but it was absolutely the best thing that ever happened to me. It forced me to deal with an issue I never would have addressed on my own. Now, this was not the way I expected Randy to show his love for me, but discipline is a genuine form of love. God will give your husband discernment on how to handle you—and I thank Him for that.

THE BATTLE FOR THE FAMILY

Randy: Family life is under attack like never before. The divorce rate is on an alarming increase. We used to say the statistics show that half of all families are broken by divorce, but it's more than that now. I no sooner marry a couple than I have them in my office for counseling because they're on the verge of separation or divorce.

Why? People are not willing to listen to wise counsel. You can tell somebody, "You don't want to do that"—but they're going to do it anyway. People are hardheaded. Sit in my office and wear my shoes, and you will see.

We don't show our true selves to one another before the commitment is made. Then down the road, we wonder why we're being asked to change. That spouse of yours wants you to change because he or she has never seen the real you, and there are some things about you that aren't all that attractive.

The Word of God has the only successful formula for a happy marriage. Men like to think it begins with the "S" word—submit. As Paula mentioned, we're going to really get into that later on in the book, but it's true that wives are to submit to their own husbands as they would to the Lord. You wouldn't get puffed up, arrogant, and talk back and snap your fingers at God, but you have no qualms about doing that to your husband.

The Bible is clear that the husband is the head. He wears the pants in the family. But this position carries responsibility with it. Husbands are responsible for their wives and their children. Where are the men of the church today? In the body of Christ, women do 90 percent of the work. Men are not taking their rightful position in the church or in their homes.

The world has a lot of theories about marriage and family issues. But the nuts and bolts of what makes a family work needs to be taught in the church, and it isn't being addressed nearly enough. We live in a "playboy society" where if it feels good, do it, and don't worry about the repercussions. We just step out and do what we think we want to do without allowing anybody to speak into our lives and give us any wise direction.

Therefore, we are watching many, many marriages split apart. The devil wants to destroy you through your family. Many times, family members can say something to us that cuts us to the quick faster than anybody because they know exactly who we are. We must not allow the structure of the family to become so casual and unorganized that it loses its strength and stability. And family members must never be allowed to treat each other with disrespect and lack of dignity.

The church is only as strong as the family unit. We need to love and respect one another. We need to thank God for families that come to church together.

If you have a teenager living under your roof, get him or her into church with you if you have to drag him or her by the hair. If they're eating your meals, driving your car, and using your air conditioning, the least they can do is have enough respect for you to get up out of that bed and go to church with you.

If they're lording it over you now, what do you think they're going to do when they get a little older? So what if they tell you they don't want to go to church or school. You make them go. I don't care if they sit there and pout through the whole service or the entire school day, you see that they go.

Don't think you aren't accountable, parents, for your teenager who is going to hell while you're sitting in church with your Bible in your lap.

We'll talk more about the family in chapter six. Right now, we need to talk about the third "F"—finances.

Finances

I believe with all my heart that if you don't tithe, you can't expect much in the way of blessing, but one thing I want to make absolutely clear is that God does not have a problem with Christians having money. In fact, God doesn't have a problem with Christians being wealthy. Deuteronomy 8:18 AMP says, . . . *for it is He [God] Who gives you power to get wealth, that He may establish His covenant which He swore to your fathers, as it is this day.* If God had a problem with Christians prospering financially, He wouldn't have given you the power to get wealth. God has no problem with you driving a nice car or living in a nice home. What God does have a problem with is the cart coming before the horse, so to speak. Matthew 6:33 AMP says, *But seek (aim at and strive after) first of all His kingdom and His right-eousness (His way of doing and being right), and then all these things taken together will be given you besides.* He does this so that He might establish His covenant with us.

Then when God begins to bless you, people notice and ask what's going on. "What's your secret? How did you get that new house? Check those clothes out!" That's your opportunity to say, "God is a good God. My children are not sick. I'm in my right mind. I am in covenant with the most high God."

The Bible says you earn your living by the sweat of your brow (see Genesis 3:19). It also says that a man who does not provide for his family is worse than an infidel or unbe-liever (see 1 Timothy 5:8). If I had to flip hamburgers at Burger King to make sure my wife and family were taken care of, I would. If I had to sell newspapers on the corner at three o'clock in the morning, I would do it. But you would be amazed at the people who have no work ethic. Some think they're called to the ministry and say, "Because I'm called into ministry, I don't have to work." Baloney!

Despite what so-called "liberated" women may say about sharing the responsibilities of making a living for the family, I often hear an entirely different story in counseling sessions. Many wives have confided their feelings of resentment about having to re-enter the marketplace, especially if it is an absolute necessity. Even having to work part-time bothers many wives if their income is required to help meet basic, day-to-day living expenses.

Although lots of women claim to need a career, they are also convinced that their earnings shouldn't be counted on as a means of making ends meet. They want "their" money spent on luxuries they might not be able to afford if they didn't work, but they feel their husband's income should cover the basics: food, clothes, housing, transportation, and other necessities common to living comfortably.

Most women just want a choice. They strive for the right to have a say in whether they'll be a full-time home-maker or a career person—or the combination of both.

Paula: I agree with Dr. Willard F. Harley in his book, *His Needs, Her Needs,* where he mentions "the materialistic trend that has forced women into the work force to 'keep up with the Joneses,' not to mention just to keep up with the bank and the credit-card bills."

He says "many couples set a standard of living for themselves far higher than they need to be happy. If they would simply reduce their standard of living to a point of comfort, many could avoid husbands working long hours and wives pressured to earn a paycheck. Sometimes this single adjustment will give women the choice of career or homemaking that means so much to them."

We are not saying that married women should never work outside the home. Obviously, everyone's needs are different.

Some couples absolutely could not make ends meet without both the husband and the wife working full-time.

Randy and I are very open about this. I do very well for myself, but Randy is the head of our home. I manage our money only because I'm more detail-oriented than he is. However, I go to him on all financial matters, which is wise, because a man's worth stems from his ability to provide.

Randy: A man's self-esteem is critically linked to his ability to provide for his family. In premarital counseling sessions, we deal with couples not just from the perspective of actual finances, but also how each individual views finances. We ask the prospective husband, "Are you a careful manager of your money? How do you spend money? Who's going to be in control of the money? Who will have the ultimate say?"

We ask the future bride, "Are you a big spender? How will you feel about someone else deciding how your money is going to be spent, saved, and invested?" These are important issues because resentment can build quickly when it comes to who controls the family purse strings. If the wife is out buying ten dresses and he thinks they should be saving, saving, saving, it's going to lead to a fight.

We talk to couples about their beliefs on tithing. We ask, "Do you view tithing as holy, as scripturally ordained?" If not, we begin to explain the roadblocks they are going to run into.

Paula: Let me also say with regard to the area of provision, these days a wife may earn more money than her husband. If this applies to your situation, you should continually encourage him, because the Bible warns that a foolish woman destroys and plucks down her own house with her own hands (see Proverbs 14:1). Do not destroy your house. Don't tear down your husband with your demeaning words because of his inability to provide.

Why can't he provide? Is it a season? Is it a disability? If he's just purely lazy and won't work, I say this to you: You're the one who married him. You should have considered what the Bible teaches before you said "I do."

Live within your means. If you're making $25,000 a year, don't try to keep up with somebody who's making $100,000 a year. It's amazing, but we can counsel people about finances until we're blue in the face, and they just don't listen. And it isn't just young people who have certain mindsets about finances. Older people view financial issues differently than some of the rest of us because they lived during the Great Depression and did without many things just to survive.

Allow me to tell a story about an elderly lady who lives with us. She was the first widow of our congregation, and Randy told her husband on his deathbed that we would take care of her, and so we do. She lived through the depression. When you talk with her, she'll tell you she's broke. She and her late husband wouldn't spend fifty cents to drive on a toll road. In fact, they would pay two dollars more in gas to avoid paying fifty cents to drive on a toll road. You can have a million dollars and still be in poverty. It's not the amount of money you have that matters—it's what you do with your money.

This couple was in agreement about finances throughout their married life, but they didn't really enjoy the financial security they had earned. Although they could have lived the abundant life God planned for them, living through the depression had caused them to be fearful that good economic times wouldn't last, so the depression lived on within them.

YOU CAN HAVE A MILLION DOLLARS AND STILL BE IN POVERTY.

Randy: **Finances can add tremendous stress to the marriage relationship when there's a lack of money or mismanagement of funds. We've talked about work and the benefits to be enjoyed from having a strong work ethic. But there's more to finances than working. Take giving, for instance. Never sell what you can sow, and you'll begin to walk in a flow of financial blessing that will never come to an end. You ask, "What do you mean by that?"**

NEVER SELL WHAT YOU CAN AFFORD TO SOW

Everybody has something to sow. There's a biblical principle called sowing and reaping. You can sow a new suit, clothes, a car. You can sow furniture. Find something and sow it. Why? Because the dividends are greater if you sow it than if you sell it. The Bible says when you give to the poor, you lend to God (see Proverbs 19:17).

Do you want to have a great marriage? Do you want to prosper spiritually, financially, emotionally, in relationships? Mentor a young, married couple. Have them over to your house for dinner. Give, give, give. Give somebody a ride to church. Take someone out to eat. Don't be self-centered or self-focused and always thinking about yourself.

Avoid financial entanglements. For example, don't ever—I mean never—co-sign a loan for anyone. Do you realize the Bible warns against co-signing (see Proverbs 22:24-27). Here's where the problem lies. Family members who see you doing well will ask you to co-sign a note for them at the bank. This kind of thing can lead to some real challenges for you personally and in your marriage.

The situation is even worse if the people wanting your help are non-tithers. If they are not tithing and you're co-signing their bank loan, you are endorsing their disobedience. Bishop Joseph Garlington, a man of God whom I respect, says he's convinced that if you mix your finances with a non-tither, it can actually contaminate your giving. Now, that's heavy!

I can never talk enough about the importance of tithing. I don't know how God does it, but He always takes the 90 percent He allows us to keep and stretches it. So give God his 10 percent. Really, everything we have comes from God—He just lets us keep 90 percent because He's so good. He is *Jehovah-Jireh*. He is *El-Shaddai*. He is not El Cheapo. Trust God. Don't fuss and fight about finances. Give as much as you can above your tithe, and watch God bless your marriage, your family, your job, your church, your relationships, and everything else in your life.

FELLOWSHIP

Paula: The dictionary defines *fellowship* as "friendship; companionship; two or more people having the same activities and interests." Your mate is your lover, but he (she) should also be your best friend. Best friends develop their relationship by doing things together that enhance the friendship. Friends stick together no matter what.

A female acquaintance of mine has many close friends, but there are three friends in particular who, she says, stick together "through thick and thin, sick and sin." These ladies are there for one another in good times and in bad. Their husbands are also friends, so the relationships are strong and solid. They have weathered many storms together, ranging from cancer to the divorce of one of the couples because a mate met someone on the Internet!

If you walk in integrity and have a pure heart, you are going to be all right no matter what the devil tries to throw at you.

Randy: **I have a favorite little phrase, "Tell your enemies everything, and they have no ammunition against you." We believe in honesty and transparency in relationships. I think the main reasons people avoid being transparent are shame and condemnation—we feel that if we're totally honest with someone, they won't love and accept us.**

Paula: Before I was saved and met Randy, I became pregnant with my son and then married his father. And I was so ashamed of that. This guilt, along with many other factors, contributed to the breakup of my first marriage. Later on when I heard the Gospel, God tremendously changed my life around. I never thought I would get married again, this time to a man of God. I definitely didn't think God could use me or call me. I didn't know much about religion at the time—I just wanted to love God.

Years down the road, it was difficult for me to fully accept the call of God on my life because of my past. A minister I highly respected came to me and said, "Paula, who in the world am I to ever judge you? God knew you would do every single thing before you did it, and He still called you. He knew everything you would go through, and He still placed His hand on your life. Who am I to judge what God has declared?"

His comments set me free. I think that's why we should be transparent. We should not fear man's opinion when we've come clean before God. I don't think we have to go into every nitty-gritty detail of everything we've ever gone through because that can be too painful. But when you enter into a relationship, basic knowledge of what's happened before is helpful.

Randy knew I'd been abused. He knew my past. It wasn't going to be a surprise that was going to disarm him and bring problems into our marriage.

Randy: **Transparency brings healing because you can honestly say, "I'll tell you all you want to know about me right now—up front." It takes the fight out of the stone throwers.**

Honesty is important in all relationships. Recognize that all people have failures and flaws—all people have gone through something, whether they wish to discuss it or not. Openness in relationships brings healing to you and also disarms anyone from ever bringing something against you.

Be prepared! Fellowship with your spouse may include trying something that you haven't felt comfortable with in the past. For instance, I like to ride Harley-Davidson motorcycles, and I like movies. Paula likes to shop. So we compromise—I go with her to the mall, and she'll go to a movie with me.

Paula: Now, for me to sit two hours and watch a movie is very difficult. Just being still for that long is a challenge for me. But I've learned to enjoy it because it is something we can share together, and I think that's important. Don't be so closed to options you haven't previously considered. Be open to trying what would please your mate. You might really enjoy it!

FUN

Randy: As busy as we are, we have a fun night every week. We go out on a date. We don't take the kids with us. Something's wrong when you must always have the children with you. I know they're part of your family, but you need to act as if you were dating once in awhile. Believe me, it refuels the fire!

I've got a Sports Utility Vehicle (SUV), and Paula and I were out one date night on a back country road. And I said, "Honey, we're going to pull over like we used to." I locked the doors, and business began to pick up.

Paula: He acted like we were eighteen years old or something.

Randy: She said, "We've got this huge house. . . ."

Paula: And he said, "But it's date night." And the fact is, one of men's most basic needs is companionship. So it's a problem when a woman is dating a man and she goes to football games with him and acts as though she loves it. She pays attention to him and what he likes. But when they get married, she doesn't want to do those things anymore. The very thing that he was attracted to, she has now disassociated from him. It's dangerous.

Randy: Can you imagine this? While we were parked on our fun night out, a policeman came knocking on the door of the SUV! Oh, well.

Paula: You should have heard his explanation to the officer!

Randy: My point here is to work at keeping romance and companionship in your marriage. Both are important to the strength and stability of your relationship. Have fun. Remember to play as hard as you work. No matter how busy your schedule, make time to spend alone together. After God, your first responsibility is to one another.

If one or both of you has to be out of town, make sure you take the time to communicate. Work at maintaining a tremendously strong trust factor with each other.

MARRIAGE CAN'T WORK WITHOUT GOD

1. **The six "Fs" that will enhance your marriage and family**
   a. Faith
      1. Faith in God is the foundation of every successful marriage
      2. Hard issues the church hasn't dealt with
      3. Women haven't had a positive example of true godly submission
   b. Fitness
      1. Take care of yourself—spirit, soul, and body
      2. The body of Christ is overweight and unattractive to the world
      3. Put God first in your spiritual priorities
   c. Family
      1. Satanic attack on the head of the house
      2. Husband is accountable to God for how a home is handled
      3. Parents are accountable to God for their children
   d. Finances
      1. The importance of tithing and giving beyond the tithe
      2. Wives in the workforce
      3. The husband as provider
   e. Fellowship
      1. Defining fellowship (friendship, common interests, etc.)
      2. Honesty and integrity in all relationships
      3. Transparency
   f. Fun
      1. Weekly date night without the kids
      2. Don't lose 'that lovin' feelin'
      3. Work hard to maintain an atmosphere of lighthearted fun

Homework Assignment

Husbands and Wives

1. Set aside fifteen minutes this week to bring your family together for devotions and prayer time. Give your children the opportunity to hear you pray for each other and for them.

2. Wife, find ways to honor your husband as head of your household.

3. Husband, execute a plan to take your wife out on a fun date. You arrange for child care, call her and ask her out like you did before you were married, and go someplace romantic. If money is tight, arrange for child care outside your home for an evening, pick up a couple of candles, and order a pizza to be delivered. Cuddle up in front of the fire and have fun!

Lord, You are worthy of honor and praise. Thank You, Father, for Your Word. I praise You that Your Word is a lamp unto my feet and a light unto my path. You are the foundation of every successful marriage, and I declare that my marriage is a success! With Your help, I commit to follow the six "Fs" (faith, fitness, family, finances, fellowship, and fun) and will enhance my marriage and family relationships. Help me to avoid grumbling, faultfinding, and complaining about my mate, my children, and my circumstances, and commit all of these to You. Search my heart and reveal my shortcomings in order that my life may become pleasing to You. In the name that is above all names, Jesus, the Christ. Amen.

three

THE "S" WORD: SUBMIT

Wives, be subject (be submissive and adapt yourselves)
to your own husbands as [a service] to the Lord. For the
husband is head of the wife as Christ is the Head of the
church, Himself the Savior of [His] body. As the church is
subject to Christ, so let wives also be subject in everything
to their husbands.

—EPHESIANS 5:22,24 AMP

Randy: If you're a wife, take a deep breath here for a minute, because the "S" word is coming up. And husband, this really isn't the time for you to run to your desk drawer for the highlighting pen so you can keep track of how many times we point out that you're in charge here and she should act like she knows it. You had better be careful because you're about to set yourself up in a big way.

Wives, submit. . . . Now, there's the word. That didn't hurt much, did it? I know we live in the feminist era, but the feminism promoted by the world is contrary to the Word of God. The analogy in Paul's letter to the church at Ephesus excerpted here is that because Christ is the Head of the church, He is the Savior of the body. And that's what Paul is saying to husbands. You are the head, you wear the pants, and you make the final decisions, but with that position comes all of the responsibility for your family.

You like that submission part, don't you, guys? When I've taught on Ephesians 5 as pastor of Tampa's Without Walls International Church, I've received lots of "amens!" at the conclusion of this scripture reading. What you have to consider, though, is that with knowledge comes responsibility. *Responsibility* is defined by Webster as "the quality or state of being responsible; moral; legal; accountable; reliable; trustworthy; answerable."

In this chapter, we're going to focus on wives being submissive to their own husbands. We're going to go everywhere we can go in the family and the home—from the kitchen to the bedroom—because if you can't talk about these things in church, the world is going to offer you instructions on them. The world has many answers, books, films—lots of material—that they would love for some unhappy spouse to get hold of and declare, "This is the way it's supposed to be done." No, sir. The Word has the only successful formula for a happy marriage.

Husbands, love your wives, as Christ loved the church and gave Himself up for her, so that He might sanctify her, having cleansed her by the washing of water with the Word (vv.25,26 AMP). Paul uses an analogy again. Christ has sanctified the church. *Sanctified* means "to consecrate; to set apart for a sacred purpose; to free from sin; purify; to make efficient as the means of holiness." He wants you to do the same with your family, *that He might present the church to Himself in glorious splendor, without spot or wrinkle or any such things [that she might be holy and faultless]* (v.27).

Verse 22 presents a strong argument for wives to *submit.* It does not mean that wives are to be men's slaves. Paula and I were in a preacher's home one time—I won't tell you who, but you probably would know him. While we were there, this man sat in his recliner with his TV remote control in his hand watching sports. This guy was shouting out orders and snapping his fingers, "Get me an iced tea! Bring me some potato chips! Get me this! Bring me that!"

His wife was running like a little puppy dog. And when we left there, Paula said, "Oh, I'd have gotten those things for you, darling. You would have *worn* them."

Submission does not mean you are to treat your wife as a slave who must run and fetch like a puppy dog every time you speak. No, sir! If you've thought that was submission, you have misunderstood the word. Yes, there is a duty for the wife to be submissive, but it never means that husbands have the right to lord it over their wives. *I'm the king of the jungle! Aha!* Stick out your chest, pound your fists on it, and everybody runs. *Me Tarzan, you Jane!* It has never meant that a wife is of lower rank than her husband. It doesn't mean she lacks dignity,

Eve was taken from Adam's side. Your wife, sir, is to be equal to you. She is your help meet.

You will find that your wife can be a great comfort to you in the decision-making process, but the wife doesn't wear the pants in the family—the man has the final say-so. It's the husband's duty to say, "Enough is enough," sometimes. The buck has to stop somewhere. At some point, the husband has to say, "This is the decision I've made, and we're going to live by it."

Why? Because when the rubber meets the road—in the acid test, so to speak—it is the husband who will stand before almighty God and give an account for his family. You are pastor over your own family. If your family is out of order, you might want to check up on your spiritual walk with God.

Remember the differences between men and women that we talked about in the first chapter. Men are conquerors and women are emotional beings. Women like to nest. I can take a piece of plywood, place it on two cinder blocks, and say, "This is my bed." But Paula wants to put a picture over it. She wants to put a little lace on top of it, a little fluff, and maybe a ruffle or two because that is her instinct. Men aren't like that.

Take the mall, for example. When we men go to the mall, we're hunters: *boots . . . store . . . get.* Don't look at the price, whether it's on sale or not. Go. Bottom line. Not women. No, sir. The husband may say, "Honey, will you go buy me some boots?" Eight hours later, she's back. "Where are the boots?"

"Well, I went to Kmart. I went to Simms. I went here, I went there. I compared prices. I'm going back on Monday. I've got three more malls where I can look. And the details— she knows what every pair of boots in each store she visited looks like, how much they cost, who has some similar to the ones she liked best, and how they will look (if she ever buys them) with a certain outfit she's also picked out.

This is a woman's makeup. And you can't fault her for it. You can't hold it against her, because God created the woman this way. If you don't want to know all the details, take it up with God, because He made her.

And, women, you need to understand a man's makeup. It bores him for you to go into all the details. That's the way God created him. He just wants to get from point to point. I often say to Paula, "Please, please, get to the point." But I've found out that when the two become one, they make a beautiful couple.

... WHEN THE RUBBER MEETS THE ROAD ... IT IS THE HUSBAND WHO WILL STAND BEFORE ALMIGHTY GOD AND GIVE AN ACCOUNT FOR HIS FAMILY.

Since I've learned about the differences between men and women, I've saved myself a world of trouble by listening to my wife in that detail spirit she has—that special nature of hers. I'm not sure what it is—some say it's intuition—but I believe it's something that God puts into a godly woman enabling her to detect things faster than men.

You hear verse 22 quoted a lot, *Wives, submit.* . . . But we rarely hear a message preached on verse 25, *Husbands, love your wives, as Christ loved the church and gave Himself up for her.* One man asked, "Why did God put that in there? I like the submission part, but, oh, that part about loving her as Christ loved the church."

Paula: Many times wives fail to submit or even shudder at the word submit because their husbands have not assumed the rightful position that God called them to. You might say, "So what?" Your disobedience handcuffs God so that He cannot move in any area of your life. You can cry out day and night, "God, move in my marriage. I need a miracle in my marriage, Lord," and He can do nothing because you've been a rebel at home. As long as you're out of submission, God won't make a move.

Now, you may be thinking, *Paula, Randy, you have no idea what you're asking me to do. You don't know what this man is like. You have no idea what kind of situation I'm living in. He's a jerk. He's not affectionate at all. If I prepared a candlelight dinner and was dressed in a sexy negligee when he came home, he'd still head for the den and want his dinner served on a TV tray without even looking at me.*

And I hear you, husband, saying, "Are you kidding? When I get home, the house is a mess, the kids are screaming, the sink is full of dirty dishes, and she's lying on the couch in the robe she had on when I left this morning, looking exhausted."

Well, first of all, we're not asking you to do this—God is. Let's see what 1 Peter 3:1,2,7,8 AMP says, and we'll spell out exactly what we (husbands and wives) are to submit to.

> *In like manner, you married women, be submissive to your own husbands [subordinate yourselves as being secondary to and dependent on them, and adapt yourselves to them], so that even if any do not obey the Word [of God], they may be won over not by discussion but by the [godly] lives of their wives, when they observe the pure*

*and modest way in which you conduct yourselves, together
with your reverence [for your husband; you are to feel for
him all that reverence includes: to respect, defer to, revere
him—to honor, esteem, appreciate, prize, and, in the
human sense, to adore him, that is, to admire, praise, be
devoted to, deeply love, and enjoy your husband].*

*In the same way you married men should live
considerately with [your wives], with an intelligent
recognition [of the marriage relation], honoring the
woman as [physically] the weaker, but [realizing that you]
are joint heirs of the grace (God's unmerited favor) of life,
in order that your prayers may not be hindered and cut
off. [Otherwise you cannot pray effectively.] Finally, all [of
you] should be of one and the same mind (united in
spirit), sympathizing [with one another], loving [each
other] as brethren [of one household], compassionate and
courteous (tenderhearted and humble).*

I really battled the submission thing for a while. I was like,
"You tell me to submit, man of God, but what am I supposed to
submit to?"

And I found the answer in 1 Peter 3: I'm to submit to the
godly man who is considerate, who is able to intelligently recognize what the marriage relationship is all about, who will honor
me, who knows I am a joint heir of God's grace with him, who is
united with me in spirit and is sympathetic, loving, compassionate, courteous, tenderhearted, and humble! Now, I don't have a
problem with that! I love that! How about you?

Madam, God made your husband the head over you for your
protection. It's a benefit. It wasn't laid out to hurt or control you

but to protect you. I didn't figure this out for a while because I had been abandoned and abused. So I thought Randy would eventually abandon and reject me.

I thought he said things to control me. Until I went through a devastating situation that God used to open my eyes, I didn't believe Randy was there for my protection—to keep me from harm. I learned that God had positioned him as the head of our household for my safety. When I understood this and began to receive God's truth about Randy and me and our situation, I could walk in submission. Randy was trying to love me as Christ loved the church—unconditionally—but I wasn't cooperating.

Christ gave His life for the church (you and me), and when Randy loved me unconditionally, there came a trust factor and a safety element to our relationship.

Randy: **Here is a perfect example of what we're talking about. We got into an argument about something in the drive-through at Steak 'n Shake one day.**

Paula: It was Boston Market.

Randy: **I didn't know Boston Market had a drive-through.**

Paula: It doesn't matter. I submit to whatever you want to think it was because it's irrelevant. Let me show you something about the differences between men and women. That's the whole point—it doesn't matter if it was Boston Market or Steak 'n Shake. The point is you were going to talk about our argument. Just helping you out, baby.

Randy: Lay hands on her. We pulled up to this drive-through, and we were arguing. We were going at it—I mean, really fighting. Suddenly Paula said, "Well, I'll just get out." And I said, "Get out." So she got out of the car, and I pulled away.

As I started to pull off, literally, this is what she did. She jumped on the hood of the car as I was driving down the street! I am not kidding! I turned on the windshield wipers, and she was holding on to them, going back and forth.

You see, her thoughts had immediately reverted to her childhood when her daddy had abandoned her by committing suicide, and later she was abandoned by her stepfather. She didn't want to be abandoned by me, so she jumped on the hood of the car and held on!

This happened right after we moved to Tampa from Washington, D.C. Since then, she's been delivered. Thank You, Jesus.

Paula: There is an important point to make right here. Identify the *why* behind the *what*. I could fight with Randy all night long, but he'd better never leave me. Why? Because the night my dad committed suicide, he grabbed my mother's arms and began to beat her head in. He said, "If you don't give me Paula, I'll kill myself."

He did exactly what he said he would do. So, in my mind, I did not consciously recognize that fear came in when Randy and I fought—fear that he would leave just like my daddy had done, and I'd never see him again. Once I was able to identify why I jumped up on the car and wouldn't turn loose, I could say, "Okay, everything's going to be all right. He isn't going to abandon me."

(Later, I realized how dangerous it had been. But isn't that how we get ourselves into dangerous situations? I was up there, hanging on, and thinking, "Now what am I going to do?")

One day Randy and I were fussing about something, and he got very quiet. Finally he said, "Paula, when are you going to get it through your mind? You may make me miserable and grumpy, but I'm going to grow old with you." I ran out of the room crying, but suddenly it dawned on me. It was like a light bulb went on inside my head. God said, "Paula, he's My gift to you." And I realized that our relationship was sealed from above. We didn't catch each other with some deceiving ploy that we'd have to continue to keep one another. God had put us together. And God was ultimately going to be responsible.

I hadn't just gone out and "caught" Randy White. God had brought him to me. I guess I had felt unworthy to keep him, and God just did so many great things in my life to help me realize and recognize His intervention in my life. Wholeness came with that revelation, and I could honestly love Randy with the complete security of knowing we'll be together forevermore!

It is vitally important for couples to recognize why each person does what he or she does and come to a healthy compromise with each other.

SUBMIT TO YOUR OWN HUSBAND

Randy: **I want to point out something else from 1 Peter 3—the part about submitting to your own husband. I might get into trouble for bringing it up, but this is a problem in the** church and probably in the workplace. **Most women don't have any trouble submitting to their pastor or to their employer, supervisor, or manager.**

Paula: Here's the problem. Many of us routinely submit to someone else's husband, but the Bible says to submit to your own husband. If the pastor asked, "Would you bring me a glass of water?" you'd say, "Yes, I'll bring it right now, Pastor." *Oh, pastor needs water. Pastor needs water.* Your little heart goes pitter-patter. You can't get to the faucet fast enough!

Then you go home and your tired husband who's had a tough day at work asks, "Honey, would you mind getting me a glass of water?" And you say, "Do I look like a servant? Get your own water." You are not submitting. The Bible doesn't tell you to submit to every other man. Of course, you honor your pastor with a submissive attitude, but the Bible doesn't tell you to submit to those in other positions. You are to submit to your own husband.

You know it's true. Just an hour ago or last week, you were over at the church and running to get your pastor a glass of water, but now you can't get one for your own husband.

Sometimes after you've been married awhile, you've smelled your husband's stinky feet and his bad breath, and you lose a little respect for him. You have to bring to your remembrance the thing about him that you fell in love with and the position in which God has placed him. Then you can submit to his position as unto the Lord.

YOU ARE TO SUBMIT TO YOUR OWN HUSBAND.

When you're doing something for your husband, you're doing it as unto the Lord. I'm using this little illustration about bringing a glass of water, but I know if God himself came down from His throne, walked into your church, and asked you to get Him a cup of water, you wouldn't have the attitude that you display with your own husband.

You are to submit to your husband as you would submit to God. You come into the household of God and say, "God, I worship You with this tithe. I worship You with my praise. I worship You and work as unto You. I do it with the joy of the Lord."

Well, serve that man you married with the joy of the Lord. He might be meaner than a cross-eyed snake, but you're not doing it for him. You are doing it as unto the Lord.

This submission issue has gotten out of hand. That word doesn't mean you're supposed to walk around like a whipped puppy. Sometimes you'll feel as though your husband doesn't deserve you. He doesn't deserve your respect and admiration. He doesn't deserve to be treated like a king and priest of his home. He doesn't deserve to be submitted to as you would submit to the Lord.

He's just human. He's going to do things that irritate you. It's important for you to realize that it isn't him you're honoring so much as the position God has given him. When you understand that, then God can move in your home life, your family, and your marriage.

OH, NO! NOW I HAVE TO REVERENCE THIS MAN?

. . . Let each man of you [without exception] love his wife as [being in a sense] his very own self; and let the

> *wife see that she respects and reverences her husband [that*
> *she notices him, regards him, honors him, prefers him,*
> *venerates, and esteems him; and that she defers to him,*
> *praises him, and loves and admires him exceedingly].*
>
> —EPHESIANS 5:33 AMP

Reverence is another word I had a hard time with because every time Randy and I fought, he said, "You're supposed to *reverence* me." I felt like reverencing him, all right—right up and down his face. I know you don't ever feel that way, but that's how I reacted. I really wanted to be the woman that God has called me to be, so I got into the Word of God and asked, "What does *reverence* mean?"

In the Greek, it's *phobeo*. It means "to strike with fear; have high regard; deep respect." I didn't like this at all when I first found out. I said, "But God, what if he doesn't deserve my respect right now?" God said, "You don't honor that man. You honor the position I put him in."

God has called your husband to be the priest of your household. We're told to do two things in Ephesians 5, submit and respect. You honor the position. There are actually four commands in these verses:

1. *Submit to your husband as unto Christ.* We've gone over that. In other words, if God himself asked you for a drink, you would get it for Him. So do that for your husband.

2. *Recognize the headship of your husband*—the rank of authority that God has placed him in. You don't do that so much verbally as you do by your actions. Verbally, we say, "Oh, he's the head of the household, but I'm in total control."

Your husband has the final decision on finances. He has the final decision on the children. He's going to stand before God and have to give an account, and that's an awesome responsibility. Instead of nagging him so much and telling him what he needs to be doing, you need to pray for that man. Get down on your knees and ask God to make him into the man that God's called him to be.

3. *Subject yourself to your husband* (v.22). *Subject* means "one that is placed under authority or control; one who enjoys the protection of and owes allegiance to; owing obedience to; to bring under dominion and control of as in a superior; to predispose."

4. *Reverence your husband.* Have high respect for him. Remember he has a need for admiration and respect. Nobody can meet that need for him like you can because that's your job. It's your purpose in life if you are a wife.

LEAVE AND CLEAVE

> *For this reason a man shall leave his father and his mother and shall be joined to his wife, and the two shall become one flesh.*
> —EPHESIANS 5:31 AMP

Randy: I may be about to split some theological hairs, but you need to realize that after Johnny marries Susie, he and his bride may stay with Mom and Dad for a little while, but sooner than later, he needs to get up, get a job, and get out on his own, providing for his own family.

I understand that there are times when a couple may *temporarily* have to move in with one set of parents to get their feet on the ground. Let's face it, there are often some rocky times for those adjusting to married life.

What I'm talking about is when Johnny is thirty-five years old, and he and Susie have lived in Mama's home for fifteen years, and he's getting lazier and fatter, while Susie's out working. It's time Johnny gets kicked out and told, "I don't care where you go, but you aren't going to live under my roof anymore."

I don't know of any two families that can live together. Eventually, somebody is going to come against one of those family members, and there's going to be discord. You've chosen your mate for the rest of your life, for better or worse, for richer or poorer, in sickness and in health, until death separates you. Your mother-in-law and father-in-law have no business speaking into your life if it goes against your family, so you shouldn't be taking advantage of their hospitality on and on.

I've seen parents-in-law split more families because they didn't like the mate their darling son or daughter had chosen. You've chosen your mate, and when you get out from under all those negative words that you're constantly hearing, things will go smoother. I love my mother-in-law, but I guarantee that she could never live with me.

Why? A man and a woman—God set up this formula. This isn't set up by Randy White. A husband and wife shall cling to one another. They will rough it together. There's something about this time that can't be compared to anything else. When Paula and I didn't have two dimes to rub together, we'd call the parents. Yes, and there were a few times when we had to live with them. But there were also times when we said, "We're going out on our own. These two are going to become one. We're leaving. We're cutting these apron strings."

There comes a time when a husband has to come out from under the covering of his parents and recognize what it is to be lord over his own family. You need to learn what being the priest of your household feels like. There's divine order for the family.

Paula: There's a principle to leaving and cleaving, and that principle must be satisfied. In order to build a strong marriage, it is God's will that you leave your parents, their security and provisions, and cleave to the one to whom you are now wed. You are not married to your parents or your in-laws, and you can no longer hold onto their coattails. The two of you are to create a new family unit, independent of your parents. When you leave the nest, you're on your own.

Don't allow your parents or in-laws to meddle in your affairs. Their interference may be well-intended, but oftentimes it only complicates matters. You will never have an effective marriage or an effective family until you learn to leave and cleave. And you can't cleave until you leave!

Let me talk to you, wife, for just a moment. You just got married, you're back from your honeymoon, and you're settling in and adjusting to all the changes that have just taken place in your life. In a week or two, you have your first really big fight, and you're hurt and wounded. Your mother calls and invites you out to lunch. She says, "I can tell by the look on your face, sweetheart, that you're upset about something. What is it, baby? You can tell your mama."

That's when you start complaining about how bad your husband is. Mama is sympathetic. After all, you're her baby girl. "And wait until I get home and tell your daddy what this man's been up to. . . ." Now you've managed to get your parents all riled up against your husband.

Then you go home, and Bridegroom says, "Baby, I'm so sorry about this morning. I don't know what that was all about." You're standing there melting because he's just the sweetest, most understanding, compassionate man you'd ever want to know, and you're jumping into bed and making love. You're all goo-gly-eyed about each other again—but guess what? Your mama is mad, your daddy is enraged, and they don't like Bridegroom anymore because he hurt their baby girl's feelings.

> YOU WILL NEVER HAVE AN EFFECTIVE MARRIAGE OR AN EFFECTIVE FAMILY UNTIL YOU LEARN TO LEAVE AND CLEAVE.

Are you getting the picture? Mama and Daddy don't get over these things as fast as you got over it, and trouble is brewing. Mama is carrying offense toward Bridegroom. And you've created something that's going to be detrimental because you didn't leave and cleave.

Don't go to Mama to work out your problems! As husband and wife, there are some things you don't share with everybody else. You work them out, and you cleave to each other.

Randy: **This is good.**

Paula: Not only do we have our in-laws or our own parents to leave, but there are some friendships you will need to let go of.

Don't call your ex-boyfriend or ex-girlfriend. You say, "I'm just keeping a casual relationship, you know, making sure we keep in touch." You have to leave and cleave. The Bible teaches us to let go of the things of the past. Let go of the failures. If your ex was so great, why didn't you marry him? Why didn't he marry you? You've made a new commitment—a new relationship. It's called leaving and cleaving.

You aren't supposed to meet an old boyfriend or girlfriend at the ballpark anymore. If you want a solid marriage and you want to build the union God has for you, then you've got to cut off some things and build on a new foundation.

I'm not saying that men and women can't be friends, but men don't need to unload their personal business about their wives on the ears of a friend, male or female. And wives should never share with another person—male or female—the shortcomings of her husband.

Randy: **There's nothing wrong with guys going to the ballpark with old friends as long as there's balance. I'm talking about guy friends—not ex-girlfriends.**

Paula: Right. We're not saying you have to give up all of your old friends when you get married, but there are some relationships that won't be healthy to your new situation. I believe you'll be able to recognize the difference between those that will build you up and those that have the potential to tear you down.

MEN OUT OF POSITION

> *And I sought a man among them who should build*
> *up the wall and stand in the gap before Me for the land,*
> *that I should not destroy it, but I found none.*
>
> —EZEKIEL 22:30 AMP

Randy: We'll discuss this in greater detail in chapter five, but here's a word on the subject of men out of position in the context of submission. You can't read a book like this or hear a message on submission, and tell your wife, "I'm the head of this home, like it or not." That isn't going to work. The truth of the matter is, the wife often runs the affairs of the home, rears the children, and unilaterally makes many major decisions about the home.

But if the truth were known, that is not the desire of her heart. Women want their husbands to take a more active role in today's family. They want you to be in position as head of the house.

There is nothing worse than an arrogant, bossy, overbearing, know-it-all, throw-her-weight-around woman—except for the husband who lets her. Elijah, after calling down fire from heaven one day, ran from the mere words of a woman by the name of Jezebel the next day (see 1 Kings 18,19). I want you to know that if a woman is not sanctified and filled with the Holy Ghost, she can be meaner than a cross-eyed snake.

It's easy for a wife to submit when you continually demonstrate your love for her. If you're not showing her respect in the home—if you're not showing her love and affection (and not just when you want sex)—she doesn't want to submit. The overbearing husband who expects his wife and children to run when he says so has no right to be the head of his household. Only when the husband is willing to be last in the family can he qualify to be first.

Your wife is not some puppy dog that has to cringe when you snap your fingers. She doesn't have to walk on eggshells when you come in the door. The dog and the kids shouldn't have to run for cover just because you're home, afraid to be around you because of your ugly disposition.

You can change your nasty attitude by the power and anointing of the Holy Ghost. You don't need to pass your clock-stopping countenance down from generation to generation either. Don't say, "Well, that's the way my dad was . . . and his dad was the same way." You need to break that curse in the name of Jesus.

YOU DON'T NEED TO PASS YOUR CLOCK-STOPPING COUNTENANCE DOWN FROM GENERATION TO GENERATION—BREAK THAT CURSE IN THE NAME OF JESUS.

Your wife wants and needs love and respect from you. When you love and respect her, you can wear the pants in your family. Proverbs 21:9 says, *It is better to dwell in a corner of the housetop, than with a brawling woman in a wide house.* I didn't write it, I'm only the mailman. I'm just giving you God's Word. It means that it is better to dwell in a shed in the backyard, in a shack somewhere, or up on a flat roof without protection from the weather, than to live with a brawling woman in a large, furnished apartment.

Now, who wrote this? Maybe he didn't understand women. Wrong! This man was married to 900 women! If anybody was qualified to write about women, surely Solomon knew women. Evidently, one of his wives was meaner than a snake. And he said it's better to live in a shack somewhere with no heat or air-conditioning, no running water, and no European king-size bed than to be with this woman.

Let's look at Proverbs 27:15, *A continual dropping in a very rainy day and a contentious woman are alike.* This may sound humorous, but it means that a woman who continually nags is like a continual cloudburst or a windstorm that can't be stopped.

Our son Bradley was putting gas in the car and spilled some on his hands. He washed it off, cleaned up, and even put some cologne on. But we could not get rid of that gasoline smell throughout the entire day. This scripture means that a continuously nagging woman is like the smell of gasoline. You can't get rid of the stink.

I'm not against women in their rightful position in the home. But a woman who runs the show without letting the man be the head of the house is out of order, according to the Word. And the only thing that's worse is the man who lets her get by with it.

Men need to take their position. Make a quality decision to love and understand your wife—cultivate genuine intimacy with her. Only you can make it easy for her to submit joyfully.

ORDER IN THE FAMILY

Paula: God has a rank of authority. We've touched on it a little already, but God's order of authority is God, Jesus, husband, wife, and children. That's God's order in the household. God is a God of order who works through authority.

We need to build healthy families that survive the heat when it comes and attract the notice of the world because we came through the storm. The world should wonder, *Why can they (Christians) make it? What is it they're doing that we haven't done? They have joy. They have peace. They have healthy marriages. Their kids aren't on drugs. What are they doing that I'm not?*

Ladies, when you rebel against your husband, you are literally rebelling against God. When you honor your husband, you're honoring God. So whenever you get that attitude, and those little devils sit on your shoulder and you start snapping at your husband, you're in rebellion. God has established an order of submission and authority, and you need to get with His program.

It is heartbreaking to Randy and me, as pastors, to see our sheep come to God and love Him with all their hearts yet be miserable in their marriages. God has said He has a full plan for you—a financial plan that will prosper you, a marriage plan that will make you happy, a home life that is second to none. *For I know the thoughts that I think toward you, saith the Lord, thoughts of peace, and not of evil, to give you an expected end* (Jeremiah 29:11).

You'll have God's order in your household when you follow His book. It comes back to the submission thing. There is something built into a man that makes him need to be stroked. You need to say things that make your husband want to take his position under God and over you and the kids. Tell him, "Honey, you are looking so good. Baby, I love you. That hair is still sexy to me. I like it coming back a little bit. That shiny forehead just does something for me."

Your man can take all kinds of hell at work, with his friends, and in the neighborhood if you build him up when he comes home. You're the one who married him. There must be something good about him. Nobody made you do it. You stood up at the altar and said "I do." There was something about this man that you loved. Think back and bring to your remembrance what it was.

GOD'S ORDER OF AUTHORITY IS GOD, JESUS, HUSBAND, WIFE, AND CHILDREN.

Husband, you do the same. Don't go out and criticize your wife to your buddies. You married her. There must have been something about her that shook your tree.

Please understand that we are not saying you can never confide marital troubles to anyone. If you have a strong network of trusted Christian friends with whom you regularly share genuine prayer concerns and not just gossip, or a friend who can capably render emotional support during a trying time and remain neutral, of course, seek counsel. But most important, you can pray.

Proverbs 5:18,19 AMP says, *Let your fountain [of human life] be blessed [with the rewards of fidelity], and rejoice in the wife of your youth. Let her be as the loving hind and pleasant doe [tender, gentle, attractive]—let her bosom satisfy you at all times, and always be transported with delight in her love.* Well, there's a new command for Christians!

Do you know what the word *rejoice* means? It means to "jump around and spin wildly." The author of Proverbs says you are to be happy, jump up, spin around wildly, and rejoice. About what? Your wife (husband). Look at this, *Let her breasts. . . .* You're thinking, *Oh, my gosh, I can't believe it's in the Word of God.* I'm not reading *Popular Mechanics* here—I am reading from the Word of God. Are you paying attention to me?

We're only addressing issues according to the Word. . . . *Let her breasts and tender embrace satisfy you. Let her love alone fill you with delight* (TLB). Hello! If I were to give you the original Hebrew translation of this verse, the words are so sexually explicit that they would be rated X. That's the Word of God. The words have to do with the woman's sexual responsiveness. I am not addressing any issues the Word of God does not address.

God wants you to have a full, happy home life and marriage within His order of authority. And you cannot say, "Pastor, you can hit the domestic part, tell me about his needs and her needs, and touch on finances, but leave the bedroom out of it."

First Corinthians 7:1-3 AMP says, *Now as to the matters of which you wrote me. It is well [and by that I mean advantageous, expedient, profitable, and wholesome] for a man not to touch a woman [to cohabit with her] but to remain unmarried. But because of the temptation to impurity and to avoid immorality, let each [man] have his own wife and let each [woman] have her own husband. The husband should give to his wife her conjugal rights (goodwill, kindness, and what is due her as his wife), and likewise the wife to her husband.*

We have discussed sex as man's number-one need. We'll suffice it to say that a wife and husband must respect each other regarding lawful sexual needs, pay the matrimonial debt, and render the conjugal duty to each other in a mutually satisfying way. Fornication will damn your soul to hell, so Paul's letter to the Corinthians spells out the alternative as marriage.

Before I married Randy, I had my own life as Paula, and God saw that. Randy had his own life as Randy, and God saw that. But the minute we went to the altar and said, "I do," in God's economy, He took two and made one. You no longer belong to yourself. We're talking about order in the family. Well, this is it. This is God's order when the husband and wife are both Christians who are serving God. But what about an unsaved spouse?

WINNING OVER AN UNSAVED SPOUSE

> *And if any woman has an unbelieving husband and*
> *he consents to live with her, she should not leave or divorce*
> *him. For the unbelieving husband is set apart (separated,*
> *withdrawn from heathen contamination, and affiliated*
> *with the Christian people) by union with his consecrated*
> *(set-apart) wife, and the unbelieving wife is set apart and*
> *separated through union with her consecrated husband.*
> *Otherwise your children would be unclean (unblessed*
> *heathen, outside the Christian covenant), but as it is they*
> *are prepared for God [pure and clean]. But if the*
> *unbelieving partner [actually] leaves, let him do so; in*
> *such [cases the remaining] brother or sister is not morally*
> *bound. But God has called us to peace.*
> —1 CORINTHIANS 7:13-15 AMP

Randy: What is the order in the family when the man, who is supposed to be second in command to God, isn't a believer? Is a wife required to submit to an unsaved husband?

Paula: Jesus said, *Thou shalt love the Lord thy God with all thy heart, and with all thy soul, and with all thy mind* (Matthew 22:37). *If any man come to me, and hate not his father, and mother, and wife, and children, and brethren, and sisters, yea, and his own life also, he cannot be my disciple. And whosoever doth not bear his cross, and come after me, cannot be my disciple* (Luke 14:26,27).

According to these verses, your God and your soul come first. If your husband asks you to submit to something that would jeopardize your relationship with God, then according to the Word of God, you are not under obligation to submit to it.

Randy: Like all pastors, we have people in our church who are married to an unsaved spouse. Usually the unsaved spouse is the husband. What are you supposed to do when your husband is a heathen? Say he's involved in pornography. How does a Christian wife handle this?

Paula: As I've said, according to the Word of God, you are not to submit yourself to anything unlawful, illegal, immoral, or that would jeopardize your soul. The Bible also says that if the wife is saved and the husband is not, she is not bound to that man. It does encourage you to stay if you can, to sanctify your household because, spiritually, you take on the role of the head.

Now, you don't lord it over your unsaved husband in the natural realm, but, spiritually, you are sanctifying your home until he comes into the position of high priest of his household. You definitely are not to submit yourself to him if he's dealing with perversion, for example, and he suggests that you participate in a "threesome" (a third party added to your sexual activities)! No. That is evil and would open a door to the enemy. Submission in marriage applies to couples that are saved and serving God together.

God only supports sexual lovemaking within the confines of marriage. Sexual practices that involve another person are wrong according to Hebrews 13:4—a warning to keep the marriage bed undefiled.

First Peter 3 says a woman should be submissive, subordinate herself as being secondary to, dependent on, and adapted to her husband even if he does not obey the Word because the unsaved spouse can be won over by the godly life of his wife. How could a man not be won over by a wife who truly honors, reveres, respects, defers to, esteems, appreciates, prizes, adores, admires, praises, devotes herself to, deeply loves, and enjoys him?

If you're a woman who can be this godly toward your unsaved spouse, he would have to work very hard to avoid seeing Jesus in you, and your Savior should become irresistible to him. It is, of course, possible that he will never take the necessary steps to ask Jesus to live in his heart. What a heartbreak for the Christian wife, who dearly loves this man, to be denied the joy of knowing that he'll spend eternity with her in paradise.

We believe God will honor your devotion and commitment to stay in the marriage, sanctifying it according to the Word by your very presence, and will reward your patience and persistence in working to win your unsaved spouse for the Kingdom.

THE "S" WORD: SUBMIT

1. **Wives, submit; husbands love as Christ loves the church**
   a. Submit doesn't mean the wife is her husband's slave
   b. Husbands will stand before God and give account for their family
   c. Husbands are the head of the home

2. **Wives and the 1 Peter 3 husband**
   a. Husbands and wives are joint heirs of God's grace
   b. The attributes of the 1 Peter 3 husband
   c. Identify why you do what you do

3. **Submit to your own husband**
   a. Women submit to their employers and pastors, but rebel at submitting to their mate
   b. Four commands for wives from Ephesians 5
   c. Leave and cleave

4. **Men out of position**
   a. Husbands need to assume their rightful position as head of the home
   b. Wives who are tenderly loved easily submit
   c. King Solomon's thoughts on living with an unruly woman

5. **Order in the family**
   a. God, Jesus, husband, wife, children
   b. Rejoice in the wife of your youth
   c. You belong to each other

6. **Winning over an unsaved spouse**
   a. Submitting to an unbelieving spouse
   b. Assuming his role as head until he submits to God
   c. Staying in the marriage and holding on to hope

Homework Assignment

Husbands

1. There are eleven attributes describing a model husband in 1 Peter 3:7,8. Attempt to add two a week to your relationship with your wife, and you'll find yourself married to a new woman!
2. Keep up the good work on her thirteen tender but not sexual touches.
3. Make a list identifying reasons for any neglect you've directed toward your wife.

Wives

1. Recognize and identify situations when you've placed the wishes of others before your husband. Schedule a time to sit down with your husband and lovingly tell him you're sorry.
2. Work on avoiding every opportunity you see to correct your husband. Also, start keeping your negative comments about him in your prayer closet.
3. Reverence your husband. Look for an opportunity to defer to him this week.

Father, thank You for bringing clear understanding where the subject of submission is concerned. I confess that I have reacted negatively to this issue in the past. I am grateful that You have poured Your love into my heart and that Your perfect love casts out all fear. I want to walk in godly love toward my mate. Lord, I make a commitment right now to believe the best of him (her). I am happy with who You created me to be. I know that You are always with me—preparing my heart to properly give and receive love. According to Your Word, I have obtained Your favor, and I believe Your will is being done in my life and in the life of my mate. In Jesus' name, I pray. Amen.

FAILURES AT
PARENTING

*Children, obey your parents in all things: for this is
wellpleasing unto the Lord. Fathers, provoke not your
children to anger, lest they be discouraged.*

—COLOSSIANS 3:20,21

Randy: Parenting is a tough subject, but one that definitely
needs to be addressed in today's world. Paul's third letter, written from prison in Rome, was addressed to the saints in
Colosse, and he also shared some guidelines for Christian families with that group, reiterating God's order of authority: God,
husband/wife, children.

Most of the problems in today's marriages—more than
half of which are ending in divorce—stem from a problem I
have identified as mutual misunderstanding. People simply
do not understand each other. They cannot meet one another's needs because they don't have a clue as to what they are.

More and more, in counseling couples about their marriage, I'm finding that the two individuals have entered the

union with problems of their own that they think will be solved by getting married. That is a mistake of enormous magnitude! Not only are their individual problems not going to go away, but marriage will only magnify them.

To illustrate, let's say one or both individuals has a problem with insecurity. Statistics show that more people are insecure than those who are secure, so when insecurity marries insecurity, guess what happens? Insecurity for both partners will dramatically increase. Insecure people spend most of their lives trying to please or impress other people. They grow exhausted with all the demands placed on them to make everyone else happy.

It's the same when there's a problem with rejection—it is only intensified by marriage. If your personal sense of well-being depends on others, your marriage is going to be in trouble right out of the blocks.

But the number-one problem in today's marriages, in my opinion, is failure to listen. In all fairness, I think most women spend a great deal of time trying to tell us what they need from the marriage relationship, but we men don't listen. Why?

We've already learned that the majority of men are head-line-oriented. We're bottom-line people. It's just the way we are. We're also conquerors. It's our nature. We set out on a trip that we've pre-determined will take a certain amount of time if we don't make any stops. When we arrive, we brag about how short a time it took for us to get there. We're about to bust from not stopping for the bathroom, but we're mighty proud of ourselves! It feels like an accomplishment to us.

When we men shop, we're hunters. We go to the mall to buy a pair of boots, head straight for JC Penney, pick up a 9-1/2, walk up to the counter, pay for them, and leave.

We don't communicate our needs to our wives because we're basically not communicators! We've already established that men are willing to speak approximately 25,000 less words per day than women! Is it any wonder we have trouble understanding one another?

Women are detailed. They have to shop at three malls, browse through every single store, and still not come home with any purchases. There's nothing wrong with that. That's how God made women. I don't understand why, but that's just the way it is.

The Bible contains everything you'll ever need to know about life—your personal finances, how to run a household or a business, your marriage, children, sickness, death, health, happiness, wholeness, righteousness, peace, and joy in the Holy Ghost. It also deals with the issues of sex. God brings a man and a woman together in intimacy for pleasure, to procreate, and to make spiritual warfare.

The Word tells husbands and wives to love their spouses, but many times they don't know how because they have never experienced love. Many men have never known that it is okay to express affection because they didn't have an affectionate father or they were raised in a macho environment where women were treated as inferiors. They really believe that if they've ever told you they love you, that one time should be sufficient to satisfy you. Most men honestly don't have the slightest inkling about how to show affection.

This is a real problem in light of the fact that women name affection as the number-one need they have in the marriage relationship. Affection symbolizes security, protection, comfort, and approval to women—all very important characteristics in their estimation.

Most men's needs for affection are minimal, and almost all men need some help in learning how to be more affectionate—but it can be done. Your wife will tell you and show you all the little things that will enhance your relationship . . . *if you'll just listen.*

Wives, I'm not letting you off the hook. How painful can it be for you to go to a ball game with your husband? Believe me, that's a way for you to demonstrate your affection for him. Does that sound too farfetched? If you just try, both of you can develop a few habits that will take you to all the places you want to go in your marriage. Come on, get with it!

AFFECTION SYMBOLIZES SECURITY, PROTECTION, COMFORT, AND APPROVAL TO WOMEN . . .

Men and women who weren't raised in a home or church where these things were taught and discussed have no understanding—not even head knowledge—of the love God has for them. That's a good place to start. How can you know how to love if you haven't even received the love of God, your Father and Creator?

So what if you heard John 3:16 read to you in church—about God so loving the world that He gave His only begotten Son so that if you believe it, you'll have everlasting life. But if these are only words from a book, you don't really know anything about love. You don't understand what all the fuss is about anyway. After all, you're here and you're okay. Aren't you?

On the other hand, when you have studied and acquired knowledge about God's love for you, it produces a confidence and security that diminishes, if not eliminates, the need to constantly have someone telling you how pretty or handsome you are, how wonderful you are, what a great cook or mechanic you are, and how super you are at this or that. You know who you are. You were wonderfully and fearfully created in the image of Christ Jesus.

When you get into God's Word, pray, and study the things of God, you will discover what a wonderful counselor He is. God is always available—24-7-365. You don't even need an appointment! God can and will help you if you'll call out to Him for help.

TRADITIONAL FATHERHOOD HAS BECOME A THING OF THE PAST

More single mothers are giving birth than ever before in the history of this country. More than 30 percent of all babies are now born outside of marriage. Why? Teen moms make up the majority of these statistics because they're desperate for acceptance, love, and attention. If sex is the only way they can have these needs met, they go for it. A young girl will find another male to provide her with the attention she craves when she hasn't received appropriate love from her father.

Beyond the alarming teen pregnancy rates, many upwardly mobile professional career women are opting for parenthood without benefit of marriage. Science has made such advances in reproductive services that men and women no longer even have to know (and I don't mean that in the biblical sense) each other to produce offspring. Sperm banks and in vitro fertilization clinics have opened throughout the country. Women can be artificially inseminated from a sperm bank . . . and can choose the color of eyes and hair, as well as the height and build of their little bundle of joy. They can also select from a wide range of intelligence quotients and health patterns. What this adds up to is women who no longer have a need for a husband—thus, the traditional family is left by the wayside.

We've already mentioned that divorce is tearing apart more than half of all American families. Men are abandoning their wives and families in record numbers—some just disappear and are never heard from again. And a trend toward preference for same-sex relationships obviously isn't conducive to producing and maintaining a traditional family.

These are some serious problems that seriously affect the *nuclear family*—defined as "a self-contained family unit including a mother and father and their children." How can spiritual order be restored to the families in our nation with problems as sobering as these? Satan has launched an all-out attack against the headship of the family. One pastor calls it an unholy assault against fathers, husbands, and future generations. We must combat it with the Word of God!

Studies show that an absentee father is a better indicator of whether a man will become a criminal than either his race or his economic status. Statistics reveal that 57 percent of male prison inmates were brought up without both parents in the home.

And, sadly, the men who live with their families are often weak. They don't *stand* for anything, and they don't *stand up* for anything. The Word of God teaches that men are to be strong. As

. . . MEN AND WOMEN NO LONGER EVEN HAVE TO KNOW EACH OTHER TO PRODUCE OFFSPRING.

head of the church, Jesus delegates authority to men to function, with love, as the head of their homes. Accountability is the result. Men are accountable to God for the roles we've been assigned.

Husband and father, this message is for you! Once you read this chapter, you're going to be accountable for the information you glean from it. The greatest sin of all is the sin of tolerance. Once God has dealt with you in a certain area of your life, you cannot tolerate it any longer. You must do something about changing.

For example, if we say that dishonesty is sin, we have to clean up our act. But we only think of dishonesty in terms of fraud in high places—the government, big business, the stock market, drug cartels . . . those kinds of things. But it's dishonest when you go to the grocery store and pick up thirteen dinner rolls in the bakery section, get to the checkout line, and say you have an even dozen. It's dishonest when your car has had transmission problems since day one, but one afternoon you wash it, put a "For Sale" sign on it, and tell the interested potential buyers, "I've never had a problem with this car. You ought to buy it. It's a good, dependable car."

I submit to you that there are four failures hurting this country more than anything—more than communism, crooked politicians, organized crime, and more than the common criminal walking the streets of the village, town, or city where you live. The greatest failure is the father who is not being the head of his home.

1. Failure to be head of your home

You've heard this before, but without the head, there is no vision. Why? That's where the eyes are located. Proverbs 29:18 clearly states—and I like it best in The Amplified Bible—*Where there is no vision [no redemptive revelation of God], the people perish; but he who keeps the law [of God, which includes that of man]—blessed (happy, fortunate, and enviable) is he.*

God holds the husband responsible for the marriage. He is to be the leader—the visionary—for the family. As I've said before, there's nothing worse than a henpecked husband unless it's the husband who allows his wife to get by with it. This may sound strong, but there is no place in God's Kingdom for that kind of man. The man who refuses to take his responsibility as head of his household puts his wife in that position by his inaction, and his family is headed for trouble—big-time trouble!

Husbands need to live according to Joshua's principle, found in verse 15 of chapter 24, . . . *as for me and my house, we will serve the Lord.* Despite what we've heard for the last twenty-five or thirty years about women wanting to be liberated from traditional family values, godly women desire that their husbands take an active role in the family. They want you to be head of the house. They want to be involved, but they want you to make the important decisions. They want you to be all that God created you to be. Do it!

Paula: All that I can add to what Randy has said goes back to a wife's need for a strong family unit. We want our husbands to play an active role in raising our children. Fathers are enormously influential in the life of a child. When dads show little or no interest in the children, mothers tend to focus on getting him to change, so the child or children lose again because Mom's attention has shifted from them to the mate who isn't doing his job.

Good parenting requires time from both parents. Some experts suggest fifteen hours a week should be directed toward quality family time. These hours include meals together, walks and/or bike rides, attending church and church-related activities, attending sporting events, reading to children before bedtime, and more. Of course, you'll need to include the things you enjoy. Everybody is different.

Be sensible about establishing your family as a unit. Don't just run out to the bookstore and grab all the parenting books that are offered as the "conclusive answer to all your parenting problems." Pray! Pray! Pray! Be honest with God about your parenting skills. He knows all about them anyway, but He will be more responsive to your needs if you are sincere and honest with Him and with yourself.

Now, children are a blessing from the Lord, but there's a danger when we try to make that child something he was not designed to be. If you are a single mom and you try to make your child the head of your household to meet a need in your own life that isn't being met by a man or a husband, or if you're trying to turn your daughter into a sibling or a mother because that relationship was not facilitated in your life with your own siblings or mother, you've taken the wrong path.

We often place unnecessary demands on our children as a result of something lacking in our own lives that needs to be identified. Children are vulnerable and easily molded. An excellent way to look at parenting is to see that God has given you a piece of pliable clay. You are responsible for designing that clay—especially in the first five years.

What goes into your children will ultimately come out. That little mind is like a computer—what you program in is going to come out. A very popular book entitled, *All I Really Need to Know I Learned in Kindergarten,* by Robert Fulghum, hit the bookstores several years ago. There is so much truth in just that title alone.

I believe our environment—what's happened to us and the experience in life—impacts us tremendously. Interesting studies have been done on groups of newborn infants. In one study, half of the babies were nurtured, caressed, and cared for in a tender, loving manner for thirty days. The other half were touched only to be changed and fed—their basic needs were met, and that was all.

The developmental differences in those infants were very significant. I think this is extremely important information, because we are placed in a position as parents, and understanding this role is critical to the ultimate outcome of our future generations.

2. Failure to properly discipline children

Randy: Notice I did not say failure to discipline your children—I said failure to *properly* discipline your children. That means you don't embarrass or belittle them and walk around with a superior attitude that says, "I'm Super Dad, and I have authority over you!" The key word is *properly*. It means "marked by suitability, rightness, appropriateness, befitting, correct."

> *Chasten thy son while there is hope, and let not thy soul spare for his crying.*
>
> —PROVERBS 19:18

The Amplified translation says, *Discipline your son while there is hope, but do not [indulge your angry resentments by undue chastisements and] set yourself to his ruin.*

My dad spanked me. Now, I realize that it is no longer politically correct to spank children or apparently to discipline them in any physical way. You can write me a letter about it if you feel the need to do so, but I believe in spanking. Just stay with me here—I'm going to bring some order to this subject.

Like me, you've probably been through this scenario as a kid—the parents would yell at you, you'd start crying, and they hadn't even touched you yet. Don't listen to the crying child. Chastise him while he's in his early, beginning years . . . while there is still time to make something out of him.

This goes along with Proverbs 22:6, *Train up a child in the way he should go: and when he is old, he will not depart from it.* Let me tell you something, my mother used to spank me too, but I never minded her spanking me. She'd yell, but her bark was much worse than her bite. But if she said the words, "When your father gets home . . ." I knew I was in a serious fix. I knew it was time for old Randy to go pick some flowers for Mom. It was time to remind her of all those favors I'd done for her—washing the dishes, vacuuming the floors. Why? Because Dad was going to take care of business—mine—and it probably wasn't going to be pretty.

He that spareth his rod hateth his son: but he that loveth him chasteneth him betimes [early].

—Proverbs 13:24

I firmly believe, Mom and Dad, that if you take care of your kids early, you won't visit them in the penitentiary when they're older. The problem with a lot of our youth today is that they don't have a positive male role model who says, "This is the line. If you cross it, these are the consequences." If you start out being a dad who says, "Today we're going to clean up some things in our household. You've talked back to your mother one too many times. Now go to your room. Dad's going to take care of you."

. . . IF YOU TAKE CARE OF YOUR KIDS EARLY, YOU WON'T VISIT THEM IN THE PENITENTIARY WHEN THEY'RE OLDER.

We need more men in the church today who are willing to stand up and be the spiritual as well as physical head of their household. It's not a popular message, but looking at today's society easily and quickly shows that many of the troubles we have with our children and youth are the direct result of a lack of strong male leadership in the home. Where are the men of the church today?

I understand that we need to bring balance in the area of discipline. We live in a society where child abuse is out of control. You must not go to extremes and beat your children half to death! There's a *proper* way to discipline children.

When I talk about being disciplined as a child and administering discipline to my own children, I'm not talking about abuse. I recognize the need to educate people about how to discipline properly, but a hand applied to a child's posterior works wonders. My dad used to have something called the "Board of Education." And every now and then, he and I had a board meeting.

I may receive some criticism about the position I take on discipline, but I am a pastor and preaching the gospel today because I had a father who knew what it was to discipline me when I was out of order. I am the leader of an international ministry that is making a difference in my city because my mom knew how to draw the line. Train up a child in the way he should go and you'll never regret it!

If you've made mistakes in the way you have punished your child or children in the past, don't be afraid to say, "I made a mistake. I've learned the proper way to discipline you, and I won't be doing it in the way I've done it before. I was wrong, and I'm man (or woman) enough to say I was wrong." Your children will respect and appreciate you for being honest with them.

Paula: I read recently in a women's magazine that 48 percent of women get their joy and fulfillment out of their children. This statistic may sound harmless to you and me, but it can place inappropriate expectations on our children—pressure, if you will—to be something they were not meant to be.

Unrealistic disciplinary measures, for example, say more about you as a person than you are probably willing to admit. Before you find yourself out of control in the area of discipline, it would be wise to identify what's going on inside you that caused such a response. Children have an innate desire for parental approval and acceptance. They really want to live up to our expectations because they define that as love.

It goes back to parental responsibility. The solution to child abuse is wholeness. One of the things Randy and I always pray is, "God, make me the wife/husband and mother/father that You intended me to be." Why do we pray that way? Because we recognize through study and just life in general that we are a product of what's taken place in our own lives.

We perpetuate behavior that we've observed in our own homes at an early age.

3. Failure to be a spiritual example

Randy: To say one thing and live another is hypocrisy. Paula and I have a little saying, "Little ears are listening." You would be amazed at what children pick up. We have to be careful what we say and do in front of them. Parents punish their children for cursing and then go out and do the same—loud enough for the kids to hear it! We tell them church is important, but we don't show up on Sunday night.

There was a great commercial on TV several years ago that showed a little boy doing everything his dad did. The dad picked something off the tree. The little boy picked something off the tree. The dad picked up a rock and skimmed it across the lake, and the little boy did the same thing in exactly the same way. Then the dad lit up a cigarette, and the little boy. . . .

Dad, the best example we can ever give is a life of serving the Lord Jesus Christ. Before you teach your son how to make a free throw, before you show him how to play eighteen holes of golf, before you do anything, you'd better bring your son to the house of the Lord Jesus Christ and let him hear you say, "As for me and my house, we will serve the Lord."

Many men were taught by example that the wife sees to any spiritual training in the house and also handles all the household chores, while the dad does nothing beyond providing a living for his family. "Do as I say and not as I do," is an old, worn-out cliché. You set the example. Many of us would never think of openly cursing, running around on our wives, smoking, drinking, or using drugs, lying, or cheating. Yet we have other bad habits.

The dad who regularly leaves his clothes strewn on the floor teaches his children to be sloppy, and it tells his children that, in his opinion, it's Mom's job to clean up after everybody. Wrong!

The dad who wants his children to grow up with good table manners doesn't sit at the breakfast table burping, scratching, sniffing, and picking! Are you hearing me? Children watch our example. They even watch what we wear.

You would be amazed at the impact you have on your children. We want our children to respect authority, and yet we get in the car with them after church and say, "How can that preacher preach a message like that? What is wrong with that man? Now, you know, this isn't right."

How can your children have respect for authority when you don't have respect for the man of God? You're sowing seeds. The dad who never has time for devotions or prayer with his children is sowing seeds. And he's going to reap a harvest—but he won't be happy with the harvest he reaps.

I'm a happy dad. Perhaps you are too. We're happy to provide a nice home, good schools, dependable transportation, and fashionable clothes for our children. But if we fail to teach our children properly through discipline and example, and they grow up to be doctors, lawyers, astronauts, bankers, and CEOs who don't know Jesus, we have failed. If they live in the finest house and get the best education money can buy, we have still failed if we neglected to bring them up in a Christian home.

Paula: What we say is important, but what we do is much weightier and carries so much more credence. Ultimately, your children and mine will be products of our lifestyles and behavior. We will win our children to the Lord by the way we conduct our lives, how we carry ourselves, and by the way we behave.

We send a loud-and-clear message to our children when we "play church" on Sunday and don't "live church" the rest of the week. We become master hypocrites (the word *hypocrite* in the Greek means "a theatrical person who wears a mask that is painted half black and half white") because we aren't real. When we fuss and fight all the way to the church parking lot, screaming and yelling at our kids about whatever, and then turn on the charm to the parking lot attendant, our kids see that we respect others, but not them.

Listen to your kids and pray for patience to understand their behavior in the different stages they go through in this thing called life. Be consistent in your walk with the Lord, and they will see the benefits of that consistency.

4. Failure to set priorities

But seek ye first the kingdom of God, and his
righteousness; and all these things shall be added unto you.
—MATTHEW 6:33

Randy: If you gain the whole world and lose your family, what has it profited you? Say you're making a six-digit salary, living on Bay Shore Blvd., and driving the latest model Mercedes. You feel successful and you look successful, but your kids hate you. Hello! There's something wrong in the family when a mother can't talk to her daughter and a son can't talk to his father.

If you allow bitterness, envy, strife, and discord into your spirit while you're out in the world "making it," it will manifest in your physical body and in your family life every single time. That's the reason some people are sick. They can't get rid of the bitterness. They can't get rid of the hatred. They've climbed the ladder of success by stepping on someone else's hands, and they're spiritually bankrupt. When they get home with their big paycheck, nobody wants to be around them because they're angry, irritable, tense, and just generally unpleasant in every way.

IF YOU GAIN THE WHOLE WORLD AND LOSE YOUR FAMILY, WHAT HAS IT PROFITED YOU?

Jesus gave His blood to forgive you, but you're still holding a grudge. You didn't get the raise you expected. That big promotion you saw coming six months ago hasn't manifested itself yet. You've re-financed the house to the max to buy a family vacation cottage at the beach, and now you're in financial trouble.

Your kids don't care if you make a six-figure salary. If driving a Ford instead of a Mercedes meant that you'd come home earlier and be in a better mood when you got there, that's what they would prefer. They want you. They need you, Dad! You'd better make things right with your wife and children. There cannot be discord in the home. The dad who puts his work, TV, sports, hobbies, etc. before his wife and children is wrong.

You may think two hours in church on Sunday morning covers your "family time" for the week, but what about the other 166 hours the kids are around? You need to teach your children to pray.

Our son Bradley knows that when I discipline, he's in serious trouble. One time I said, "Brad, Daddy's going to spank you." When I spank, I spank. I spanked him, and then I hugged him. Then I said, "Now get on your knees and pray and ask God to forgive you." He said, "Dear Lord, forgive me," and he got up. I said, "Get back down there." Tears were streaming down his face by then.

I said, "Now, Brad, get in there and read the Word. You read all these wrestling magazines and watch all this wrestling stuff on TV—you can do all of these things that add nothing positive to your life whatsoever. Well, right now, buddy, you get in there and read the Word."

If you train up a child in the way he should go, he may resent it now, but you can ask Bradley Charles today who disciplines him, and he'll say, "Daddy." If you ask him, "What happens if you do this or that? What happens if you cross the line?" Bradley will say, "This and this."

Set priorities, Dad. Golfing is not the most important thing for you to do every Saturday and Sunday. Working for the almighty dollar is not the most important thing either. Men must take their rightful position in the home.

Wives need to learn to chill out, slack up, and let their husband be who he is supposed to be. Paula and I have a marriage that is a ten on a scale of ten. I mean that sincerely. I am in love with my wife. She's what makes my heart beat. I see her, and I just go crazy. I smell her perfume, and my knees get weak. To wake up in the morning lying next to her is like I've died and gone to heaven. There's an angel beside me.

But do you know what means more to me than anything? It's not when she comes up and says, "You did a great job on your sermon today." Or when she says, "Look at how the church has grown. Look at the building. Everything really has worked out just like we planned." No. It's when we're all by ourselves, just kind of kicking back in our blue jeans and tee shirts, and she'll just do that little Paula thing that she does. She'll say, "I love you, Randy. I respect you."

When she says, "I respect you," I say, "Honey, what do you want?" She says, "The credit cards." When she says that,

I'm like a cup of drawn butter. She is saying she appreciates the fact that she and our children are my number-one priority.

I'll just break it down. Our ministry is extremely successful. God has been very good to Paula and me. She has more speaking engagements than she knows what to do with. We'll be booked up for the next two years. We recently flew up to meet the president of a large corporation to negotiate a deal to buy his building. We sat down and spoke with him about many millions of dollars' worth of property. God has been good to us.

But if I obtain all of this and lose my wife and children, what has it profited me? If I get it all, and my children grow up resenting me for not being around when they needed me most, what good is it?

A while back we were in Hawaii. We had been invited to speak at the church of a pastor friend of ours. He and his wife took care of our airfare, all of the expenses, and put us up in the penthouse suite in a deluxe hotel. It was nice. I like Hawaii. We took the elevator up to our big, spacious, beautiful suite, and I opened the curtains at the wall of windows overlooking the beach.

I said to our son, "Bradley, open the door to the balcony." He opened the door to this breathtakingly stunning view of the beach and ocean. The color blue in Hawaii is bluer than anyplace else in the world. And the greens are greener. It's just a gorgeous place, and I said, "When you're faithful to God, and you're called to the ministry, this is the kind of reward you get."

Now, why did I say that? I don't want my son growing up resenting the ministry that took his daddy. I want him to see that there are some rewards—some perks—involved in giving your life to the Lord to be used for ministry. I want him to know it's a good life, and you don't have to grow up resenting it.

Too many preachers' kids today are shacking up in hell-holes—they're out in bars, and they're sticking needles in their veins because their dad is too busy. His priorities are out of order! This principle also applies to your occupation—whatever it may be.

You may ask, "Pastor, do you have the perfect home?" Oh, no. You ought to be around our house sometimes. It's a pretty interesting place. Do you know what I like? We don't put on facades. We're real. Paula gets mad at me sometimes, slams the door, and if I'm not watching, she'll even throw something at me occasionally.

But the closest relationship we have is not in a physical, sexual way (and we're healthy in that area), but it is when we get down on our knees, and I say, "Lord, touch my wife. I love her, Lord. She's my help meet. God, I have inadequacies and failures as a husband and father. Lord, will You help me in those areas?" And

REALIZE BEFORE IT'S TOO LATE THAT YOUR KIDS WILL BE GROWN UP AND GONE BEFORE YOU KNOW IT.

she prays for me. I want you to know, the Holy Ghost will take up residence in your house if you'll do this. It is the most wonderful, intimate time.

I will not back off from what I've said in this chapter. It's in the Word, and the Word works. Get in the Word of God and study it for yourself. There would be far fewer problems in the home if men would take their rightful place and not spare the rod and spoil the children.

Pay attention to your priorities, parents—and men especially. Realize before it's too late that your kids will be grown up and gone before you know it. It seems like yesterday when our kids were just little babies, and they're growing up every day into the adults they will become in too short a time. Don't be a dad who looks back and regretfully thinks about what you should have done, where you should have been when this or that happened, or what your kids would be like as adults if you had been the kind of dad they needed.

Do what you can do while there is still time. You know what they say—you never get a second chance to make a first impression. It may be a successful business maxim, but it applies equally well to our families. I know it applies to mine. How about yours?

FAILURES AT PARENTING

1. **God's order of authority**
   a. God, husband/father, wife/mother, children
   b. A lack of knowledge and understanding
   c. Four damaging failures that are affecting America

2. **Traditional fatherhood: a thing of the past**
   a. Spiraling unwed pregnancies
   b. Absentee dads and prison statistics
   c. Men are accountable to God for families

3. **Failure to be head of your home**
   a. God gives the head or leader the vision
   b. Refusal to act as head of the home forces the wife into position
   c. Wives want husbands to make the important decisions

4. **Failure to properly discipline children**
   a. Correct ways to let your kids know who is in charge
   b. Striking the balance
   c. Spanking? Right or wrong?

5. **Failure to be a spiritual example**
   a. Little ears are listening . . . to you!
   b. Dad sets the tone for children's respect for Mom and home
   c. Success is not defined by occupation

6. **Failure to set priorities**
   a. Family life suffers when Dad's job is priority number one
   b. "Things": how important is material wealth?
   c. Developing respect in your wife and kids

HOMEWORK ASSIGNMENT

Fathers

1. Set aside time to give your children your undivided attention. Plan on working up to a minimum of fifteen hours of time a week to spend with your kids (this may include their sporting events).
2. Write each of your children a note, expressing how much you love them and how grateful you are to be their dad.
3. Take a moment to explain to your child (children) the consequences of their actions that you do not approve of, and follow through. Remember: no unreasonable responses allowed!

Mothers

1. Look for something positive to say to your children. Try to get through an entire day this week without pointing out his or her failure to meet your expectations.
2. If you need thirteen touches to feel secure and happy, think about what thirteen touches will do for your daughter. Get started!
3. If discipline is required for an infraction this week, make sure you and your husband discuss it first. Let Dad explain to the child the consequences of his/her infraction and support his decision.

Lord, teach me to listen. I confess that I need Your help to wisely prioritize my schedule so that I am open and available when my mate and/or my children need to talk. I'm trusting in You, Father, with regard to my family. I cast all of my care upon You, for I know that You care for me and those I love. Forgive me for failing to properly discipline my children, and help me to let go of any unrealistic expectations I may have where they are concerned. I ask that You give me the courage to admit my mistakes to You and to them. As for me and my house, we desire to serve You, Lord. Keep us on a godly path, I pray, in the name of Jesus. Amen.

DEVELOPING RELATIONSHIPS: LOVE WILL FIND A WAY

Paula: God is concerned about every area of our lives. He gave us His incredible instruction manual, The Bible—written to our spirit man—that covers all of life . . . spiritually, physically, emotionally, and financially. God cares about us in practical ways. He isn't only concerned about us making it to heaven, but He cares about the whole you and me.

Hebrews 4:15 tells us . . . *we have not an high priest which cannot be touched with the feeling of our infirmities; but was in all points tempted like as we are, yet without sin.* The Greek word *infirmities* means "our maladies, our weaknesses." We have a high priest who cares about the things that touch us, and we can touch Him with those things.

In this chapter, we're going to discuss a very practical subject in the lives of all women. Now, men, do not set the book down or skim to the next chapter. This is information you've been waiting a lifetime to find out. In fact, this is information you'll wish you'd had revealed to you as a young boy because it would have prevented many of those headaches and heartaches you've suffered. It could have saved you a lot of wasted time, money, and energy doing the wrong things. You're going to find out the secrets of a woman's heart in this chapter!

THIS IS INFORMATION YOU'VE BEEN WAITING A LIFETIME TO FIND OUT.

KNOW AND LOVE YOURSELF

Relationships are absolutely vital to the development of the whole person. I venture to say that if you are reading this book, becoming whole is a goal of yours. We need to be whole so we can do what God has called us to do. Fragmented people cannot give what they do not possess. How can you give life if you don't have life? God wants to bring all of us to a place of wholeness so we can be effective vessels.

We've already said that in order to love others, we must first love ourselves—and to really love ourselves, we have to *know* (not just have knowledge of) the love of God. Let's look at Ephesians 3:13-21 in The Amplified Bible and glean some wisdom from the apostle Paul:

So I ask you not to lose heart [not to faint or become despondent through fear] at what I am suffering in your behalf. [Rather glory in it] for it is an honor to you. For this reason [seeing the greatness of this plan by which you are built together in Christ], I bow my knees before the Father of our Lord Jesus Christ, for Whom every family in heaven and on earth is named [that Father from Whom all fatherhood takes its title and derives its name].

May He grant you out of the rich treasury of His glory to be strengthened and reinforced with mighty power in the inner man by the [Holy] Spirit [Himself indwelling your innermost being and personality]. May Christ through your faith [actually] dwell (settle down, abide, make His permanent home) in your hearts! May you be rooted deep in love and founded securely on love, that you may have the power and be strong to apprehend and grasp with all the saints [God's devoted people, the experience of that love] what is the breadth and length and height and depth [of it]; [that you may really come] to know [practically, through experience for yourselves] the love of Christ, which far surpasses mere knowledge [without experience]; that you may be filled [through all your being] unto all the fullness of God [may have the richest measure of the divine Presence, and become a body wholly filled and flooded with God Himself]!

Now to Him Who, by (in consequence of) the [action of His] power that is at work within us, is able to [carry out His purpose and] do superabundantly, far over and above all that we [dare] ask or think [infinitely beyond our highest prayers, desires, thoughts, hopes, or dreams—to Him be glory. . . .

Paul is saying, "Look, I'm going through all kinds of tribulation. Hell's breaking loose in my life. But it's not just for me—it's for your sake also. I'm not going to faint or collapse over it, because I recognize that this test will become a testimony to you. God will get glory out of it when He makes a stepping stone out of what the enemy meant for a stumbling block."

It may be difficult to believe right now, but one day you'll look back over your life and thank God for the people who caused you pain. There will be a day that you stand up and say, "Thank You, Lord, for that person who plucked my very last nerve! Thank You for that person who almost made me totally lose it." Why? Because you're going to find out that person had a purpose in your life. God used them, perhaps more than anyone else, to shape and mold you into all that He intended for you to be. Those people may have kept you on your knees.

Notice that Paul didn't pray the storm away, but he prayed for us to grow stronger in our inner man. Think about that, because all too often we're crying, begging, and pleading with God to make the storm cease. But instead of praying it away, Paul prayed for the storm to make us stronger. He was concerned about us becoming strong enough to overcome the storm—even when the waves are crashing and about to overtake our little boat.

A supernatural peace and assurance come into your life when you know that God is in control. The Greek word for *know* is *genosko*. It is based on the Hebrew word, *yada*. It is the same word used in Genesis where Adam *knew* Eve, and she conceived Cain (see Genesis 4:1). One concordance says the word *know* is a Jewish idiom for sexual intercourse. It is intimacy.

So we're not talking about head knowledge that God loves you. We're describing the kind of knowledge that produces self-confidence and security. No matter what your kids are acting like, whether or not the dog bit you, despite the fact that you burnt the toast . . . or your husband came in and said, "I don't love you anymore"—you can still smile, put on sexy lingerie, and say, "I *know* God has told me, 'For me and my house, we shall serve the Lord.' I *know* you are going to be priest of this household. I have a promise from God that supersedes anything you're saying in the natural realm, and you can't make me angry. You can't make me jealous. You can't rob my peace.

"No, I'm not praying this storm away, but I'm praying to be stronger in my inner man so the storm cannot affect me. It cannot control me because I won't release that power to anybody. I serve a God who supersedes the natural realm. Hallelujah." This realm of confidence comes from knowledge based on the intimacy of an experience with almighty God.

You don't get intimate until you get naked

The only way you can have that kind of knowledge is to be intimate, and you don't get intimate until you get naked. You may be afraid to stand before God naked. Perhaps people have hurt you, abused, molested, and taken advantage of you. As a result of those injuries, you may look at God through the eyes of man, instead of looking at man through the eyes of God.

> "No, I'm not praying this storm away, but I'm praying to be stronger in my inner man so the storm cannot affect me."

God is not going to leave you. He is not going to abandon you like some lover that will use you and throw you aside when he's finished with you. He's never going to hurt you. He is a God who loves you and cares for you. He neither slumbers nor sleeps. When your mother and father forsake you, He will be there. He lifts you up by his right arm. He comforts you. He is the *paracletos*—the one who walks with you.

It may take some time to arrive at this place of knowing God's everlasting love for you despite other people having messed you up, but we've written this book to help you on your journey toward emotional health and wholeness. You cannot outrun the outstretched arms of God. In fact, the Bible says God is married to the backslider (see Jeremiah 3:14).

Read the Old Testament book of Hosea. It is a perfect illustration of how much God loves the church. The interpretation is generally accepted that God commanded the prophet Hosea to marry an unchaste woman, or a woman who became unfaithful, left him, and prostituted herself in order to satisfy her fondness for luxury.

Hosea continued to love her in spite of her wicked ways. He was so devoted to her that he bought her back from her pimp. Why am I getting into all this? Even if you have prostituted yourself, sleeping with anybody and everybody you could find, God's arms will still reach out to you. He will still chase you down because you cannot shake the love of God. It is not based on what you do or don't do.

He loves you with an unconditional love. You cannot earn it. You do not deserve it. You just have to get to the place where you can receive and understand this God who is described in John 4 simply as love. Doesn't that make you feel good? Just thinking about this kind of love will bring butterflies to your stomach.

God is saying, "I don't want you to just have head knowledge about My love for you. I don't want three people to have to convince you that I am who I say I am. I want you to have knowledge based upon the intimacy of an experience."

PAUL'S THORN IN THE FLESH

Remember the biblical account of Paul praying and asking the Lord to remove the thorn in his flesh? Everybody in Christendom has his own theory about what Paul's thorn in the flesh really was. Some theologians say it was epilepsy or some other physical infirmity. Some say it was a demonic force. Others say it was another person who just kept plucking at Paul's last nerve. Whatever it was, it bothered him. That's all we need to know.

Paul asked the Lord to please take it away because it was a hindrance to him. And in so many words, God said, "I'll do no such thing." Basically, God told Paul, "I'm going to leave it there because it keeps you before Me, humble in My presence—it keeps you on your knees."

In other words, God says, "I'm going to get purpose out of that person who has been a hindrance and heartache to you. There is a purpose for the storms in your life."

Why don't you just stop right now and smile about all the tribulation you've had to go through, because what the enemy meant to *break* you actually ended up *making* you. And there will be a day when you come to wholeness and say, "Thank You, God. I didn't like going through that, but it made me what I am and who I am today. And I found the character of God and hung onto the cross of Christ through all that nonsense."

ALL OF US WANT FULFILLMENT

When you get sick and tired of being sick and tired, you will cast all of your care over on God (see 1 Peter 5:7). You will seek Him, which, according to Jeremiah 29:13, is the only way you'll find Him. When you seek God with all your heart, your mind, and your soul, the Bible says He will be found of you. The only thing that makes you seek God like that is the desperation of your situation.

So He says, "Listen here, I want you to know the width, the depth, and the height of My love for you, because it is a love that passes all your ability to understand." Why does He want this for us? So we may have the fulfillment of God (see Ephesians 3:19). The only way we can have this kind of fulfillment is to know the love of God in our lives.

All of us want fulfillment, but we aren't going to find it in another relationship, money, a career, the church, our position, a title, a fine car, a new dress or a new suit. You don't get that kind of fulfillment from a shopping spree.

You will find yourself bankrupt, empty, and void if you seek fulfillment in those things, because the only way you can find fulfillment is in the knowledge of God's love for you. And you cannot love others until you love yourself because you can only give out of your own well—out of your own self-esteem.

So we obtain fulfillment from knowing the love of God for us. Ephesians 2:10 tells us this, *For we are his workmanship, created in Christ Jesus unto good works, which God hath before ordained that we should walk in them.* Think about it—you are not just the product of your mother and father. Get this scripture in your spirit, because you can't know the love of God until you see yourself the way God sees you.

... THE ONLY WAY YOU CAN FIND FULFILLMENT IS IN THE KNOWLEDGE OF GOD'S LOVE FOR YOU.

Jeremiah 1:5 declares, *Before I formed thee in the belly I knew thee; and before thou camest forth out of the womb I sanctified thee, and I ordained thee a prophet unto the nations.* In other words, your mom and dad had to be created just to have you, and they had to come together. They had to take a honeymoon just so they could be intimate enough to produce you, because God had already ordained you.

He had to get you from the heavenly realm to the earthly realm. You aren't just here to exist. It isn't important what kinds of words have been spoken over you. It doesn't matter who said you were an accident. The devil is a liar (see John 8:44). God had already created you according to the Word. You are God's product! You were created in Christ Jesus unto good works. He did not create you to be in depression or poverty. God did not create you to be sick. No! You were created unto good works.

God created you to walk in abundant life. John 10:10 in The Amplified Bible says, *The thief comes only in order to steal and kill and destroy. I came that they may have and enjoy life, and have it in abundance (to the full, till it overflows).* Let your mind begin to imagine this. God himself brought you from a heavenly realm to an earthly realm so you could walk in the abundant life of Jesus Christ and enjoy life to its fullest.

He did not say He was going to take you into good works at some point in your life. He says you were created into good works . . . *which God hath before ordained that we should walk in them.*

You're created to walk in prosperity, health, wholeness, joy, and proper relationships. That's how you were created! He didn't create you to have a low self-image. He didn't create you to feel bad about yourself. He didn't create you to survive and just barely make it through. He didn't create you for any of that nonsense.

God made you as a product unto good works and ordained it before the foundations of the earth! And He said you should walk in it. This tells me that although that is my destiny and purpose, it is my choice! Decisions really do determine destiny.

That's what Joshua 1:8 AMP is all about, *This Book of the Law shall not depart out of your mouth, but you shall meditate on it day and night, that you may observe and do according to all that is written in it. For then you shall make your way prosperous, and then you shall deal wisely and have good success.*

You can't just have positive thoughts and speak positive confessions. That's all well and good, but you also have to meditate on it. *Meditate* means to "mentally image." New Agers didn't come up with mental imaging. God said to mentally image yourself. In other words, see yourself as He sees you.

Deuteronomy 32:10 says you're the apple of His eye. Ephesians 2:10 says you are His workmanship. Do you think God is going to make some kind of fool? I don't think so. He wonderfully, carefully, precisely, and perfectly created you. You are all that and a bag of chips! You are "bad to the bone," honey. Just give yourself a pat on the back and say, "I am wonderfully and perfectly made by the Creator of the universe!"

When you begin to see yourself as God sees you, you start to feel like royalty. You are the head and not the tail. You are the first and not the last. You come behind in no good thing. When you go to the mall, you get the best parking space. When you get on the bus, you don't walk toward the back—you act like you own the bus. You're a diplomat. You're an ambassador. That means "a delegated authority representing another kingdom."

Randy and I used to live in Washington, D.C. All the embassies of foreign countries are located there. An ambassador lives at the embassy of the country he represents. They just kind of take over. They act like they own our nation's capitol.

Christians don't usually act this way. We act as though we owe the world a favor. I don't think so. The world owes something to us. The Bible says we are a peculiar generation (see 1 Peter 2:9). We are set apart. We're different. We are a breed of our own because we have been created by Christ, and we know it!

The spirit of the living God dwells inside us. The same God that created the heavens and the earth now lives in us. We are the temple of the Holy Ghost, according to 1 Corinthians 6:19. Second Corinthians 4:7 AMP says we possess this treasure—this deposit of wealth—in earthen vessels. We are perfect because Christ Jesus has saved, sanctified, and justified us. We're baptized. That means we're immersed in His power and authority. His Word is operating on the inside of us.

We can frame our world by the Word of faith, which means we can have what we say we can have. We can do what we say we can do. We can be what God says we can be according to Isaiah 55, and His Word cannot return void. We don't owe the world anything. The world should be glad we're here. The people of the world would be going to hell—fire and judgment would be falling all over them—if we weren't living here.

How do you go about changing a negative lifestyle into a positive, mental image of yourself? By speaking the Word.

Proverbs 18:21 AMP says, *Death and life are in the power of the tongue, and they who indulge in it shall eat the fruit of it [for death or life]*. The Hebrew word for *death* as it is used here means "destruction and ruin" are in the power of the tongue. You have to speak the Word of God over yourself, whether or not you feel like it.

Remember when I said our decisions determine our destiny? I have decided to follow Jesus. It is highly likely that you have too, or you wouldn't be reading this book. We have chosen to walk in the way of righteousness. James 1:22 AMP says, *But be doers of the Word [obey the message], and not merely listeners to it, betraying yourselves [into deception by reasoning contrary to the Truth]*. The word *doer* here means "an imitator or performer."

Psalm 139:14 says, *I will praise thee. . . .* That's a choice. Here is the reason why I will praise God: *. . . for I am fearfully and wonderfully made. . . .* The word *fearfully* means "with much reverence." The Hebrew meaning of *wonderfully made* is "put to difference; distinguished; distinct; or marked out."

We are different, distinguished, chosen. Think about it, we praise God because we are created with much reverence. We are fearfully and wonderfully made. If God distinguished and marked us, why can't we see it for ourselves? Because truth has been hidden from us.

Ephesians 1:9 AMP declares, *Making known to us the mystery (secret) of His will (of His plan, of His purpose). [And it is this:] In accordance with His good pleasure (His merciful intention) which He had previously purposed and set forth in Him*. In other words, when the mystery of God's will is made known unto us, that which was hidden will be revealed.

What gives you the power to change is the understanding of who you are through Christ Jesus! Can you just imagine God up there in heaven planning you and your life? You might want to look in the mirror and say, "God, You outdid Yourself when You made me. You must have spent extra time being the Master Architect when it came to creating me. I can just see You up there saying, 'Oh, let Me see. I'll make her eyes with a bit of a slant. She needs to be born into this family because those are the genes she'll need. I want that DNA in there. She should have this kind of hair. And she needs that type of personality because I want her to do something special with her life.

"'She's going to need this gifting and that talent, and she's going to need these brain cells operating more than those brain cells.'"

Imagine God saying, "He's going to need to be analytical and logical, so he must have this kind of brain cells. And I want him to be sensitive to issues that will come up with his wife and family, so I'm going to develop that in him."

Do you think your parents designed you? You are sadly mistaken. God genetically, precisely, perfectly created you exactly the way you are, according to the destiny He ordained for your life.

Psalm 139:14 concludes with these words, . . . *and that my soul knoweth right well.* This is King David talking. He's saying, "Marvelous are Your works, God, and I know it!" That is godly confidence—recognizing that you are who you are because of what God has done. If you don't esteem yourself solely on the basis that God created you precisely the way He wanted you to be, then you'll spend a lifetime trying to be what you were never created to be.

You are who you are supposed to be. Why waste a lifetime trying to be someone else? Listen, God didn't have to bring you here in the first place. The fact that you were born is a miracle!

Building on your differences

You are set apart. There isn't anyone else exactly like you. It's your differences that make you so valuable. We live in a society that tries to portray an image for us to live up to. It's really crazy because the image they portray as correct is totally false. I started observing our little teenage girls in the church. They were looking at Miss Cosmopolitan and Miss Vogue—all these beautiful models—thinking that's the only way to look.

Guess what? The portraits of these models are sent to a computer-generated photo editor who removes the cellulite and any little lines and wrinkles that shouldn't show. Computers can make anyone's photo look great!

Society seeks to make us so image conscious that we try to fit into a cookie-cutter mold that would have everyone ending up looking pretty much the same. It doesn't take into account that our differences are what make us great.

I've learned to create a certain look. I have this cute, little white-girl look. I have it down, man. I had to do the extensions. I had my hair dyed. You should see pictures of me fifteen years ago! I get on the treadmill every day because I want to have a certain figure. I hate that thing. But there's a particular image I want to project, and, unfortunately, we live in an image-oriented society.

You may not want to hear this, but 1 Samuel 16:7 says that man looks on the outward appearance, but God looks on the heart. I wish everybody just loved us for who we are—and people who really count in our lives do. But I've learned something. I didn't know how to dress, so I went to a fashion consultant. I didn't know how to put things together. I couldn't match things up well.

I have yellow skin, and I was wearing my hair tinted auburn. Think how cute it was for me to have red hair on yellow skin.

I went to professionals to teach me what to do. Why? Because I wanted to broaden my influence so I could impact people. I recognized that there are some people who could not hear or receive the gift on the inside of me because they couldn't get past the packaging.

When I go to foreign countries, I tone everything down—my hair, makeup, and clothes—because they would never receive what I have to say if I looked the same there as I look here in America. They wouldn't listen to me. Whatever it takes to get out the message, I'm willing to do it. I've learned, like Paul, to be all things to all people (see 1 Corinthians 9:19-22). With the Jews, Paul didn't eat certain meats. When he was with the Gentiles, he could chow down on bacon. He was exercising wisdom.

You know, people in churches where I'm invited to speak probably have preconceived ideas about how I'll sound. I'm sure they are surprised when this little white girl comes out sounding like a wild woman. I know I preach like a black woman. I'm not like anyone else I know! And I thank God for that.

Doors have opened in my life, not because I'm like everyone else but because I'm different from everyone else. You have to build on what makes you different. Build on the strengths God has placed in you. You are the best you there is. You are the only you there is. Appreciate and esteem yourself for who God made you to be. Accept yourself and build on that acceptance.

Nobody can be Randy White's wife like I can. Nobody can pastor Without Walls International Church like I can. Nobody can be my children's mother like I can. Why? Because that's what I was created for. I build on my differences.

BUILD ON THE STRENGTHS
GOD HAS PLACED IN YOU.

When you discover God's love, you can love yourself. Then you can love others. We are designed as a well of life. John 7:38 says, . . . *out of [your] belly shall flow rivers of living water.* You were designed to be a vessel that gives out from all that is stored up inside you. Living water is to freely flow from you. If you have a damaged view of God's love, you cannot perceive who you are or what you're supposed to do.

HAVE YOU EVER BEEN DROPPED?

We're like the dead dog syndrome spoken of in 2 Samuel 4. It tells about how five-year-old Mephibosheth became crippled as the result of a fall. Upon learning of the deaths of his father, Jonathan, and his grandfather, King Saul, Mephibosheth's nurse dropped that little boy, the last surviving member of the house of Saul, as they fled from those who would murder the child.

How many of us have a "dead dog syndrome" because somebody we trusted—somebody we felt close to—dropped us? The Bible says when Mephibosheth was dropped, he became lame or crippled. This is exactly what happens to us when we've been "dropped" physically or emotionally. We become crippled. We're relationally handicapped. The word *handicapped* means "anything that holds a person back or gives him less chance than others have; hindrance; to make things harder for."

Out of esteem for Jonathan, David not only spared Mephibosheth's life but also restored all of Saul's personal property to the child, plus he gave him a place of honor at the royal court.

David did this because he had a covenant relationship with Jonathan, his closest friend. The child asked David, "Why would you call such a dead dog as I?" He couldn't understand David's kindness and generosity toward him.

Even though he was in the presence of the king and God had done great things for him, Mephibosheth could not see it for himself because he had a "dead dog syndrome." Hear this now, God has a table for you to feast from. He has a banqueting table set up for you so you can see and taste the goodness of the Lord in the land of the living. No, you don't deserve it. You and I don't deserve anything God has for us, but He has a legal, binding contract with us. We are in covenant with Him.

Damaging relationships may have damaged your thinking about yourself. Whether it was an abusive father, a negligent mother, a contentious sibling, middle-child syndrome, or a mean schoolteacher, many of us have been wounded by damaging relationships that affected our perceptions of ourselves. And damaging relationships affect women in a greater way than they do men.

MENDING DAMAGED RELATIONSHIPS

Don't get me wrong. It's not that men don't need warmth, love, and nurturing. They do, but not to the same extent that women do. Women have different requirements and responses to love than men have. Let me explain.

In Genesis 2:15, we see that God gave a job to the man He created. Adam was happy working in Eden. He wasn't aware of any needs in his life. He didn't look up at God in the cool of the day and say, "God, I think I'm missing something. I need a wife to complete me. I really need a great night of sex." No, Adam had no idea what a great night of sex was. He wasn't aware of any physical or emotional needs. His complete fulfillment came from his job, so he felt great about himself.

Along comes Eve. She had no self-fulfillment. She just woke up Adam's wife. As we've said before, she had no mother to train her . . . no sister, mentor, manual, books, nor college education. She didn't have T.D. Jakes to tell her, "Woman, thou art loosed!" She woke up an adult woman, married to a man she'd never seen before. She was birthed into relationship.

With the fall of mankind in Eden, the situation this couple found themselves in was compounded in many different ways. Genesis 3:16 talks about God listing for Eve the consequences of her sin: sorrow will be multiplied, children will be birthed in pain, you will desire your husband, and Adam is the boss! God did this. I mean, give me a break, Lord, You created this mess I'm in.

Let's look at this part about Eve's desire for her husband and Adam being given the position of ruling over her for the rest of her life. He's telling Eve that she is going to be relationship-oriented. That's why when women go out with friends, one of the women will say, "I'm going to excuse myself and head for the ladies room. Would anyone care to join me?" All of the ladies at the table follow in procession toward the ladies room. Men wouldn't dream of doing that. Women flock to restrooms because we're relationally oriented. We need each other.

In Genesis 3:17-19, God lets Adam know how the fall is going to affect him. He's going to be a farmer trying to till soil that's been cursed. Adam will have to work hard (the Bible says he'll sweat until his dying day to master it) to get the land to produce bread for their table. But it's a job, and Adam was created to be productive.

Women have a desire to give and receive love, but they aren't born knowing how to do that. It must be developed. Unfortunately, development is based on what we've been exposed to—and more often than not, what we saw was so dysfunctional that it isn't worth repeating. So we go on behaving in ways that produce damaging results in our relationships.

The individuals involved in those relationships will have a distorted and damaged view of healthy relationships. Why? We keep doing things a certain way because it's all we know to do. It's all we've seen our parents do. That's what our grandparents did. We have to break that cycle and develop healthy relationships according to the Word of God.

How we relate to others influences our perception of God. And how we relate to God affects how we relate to ourselves because, remember, we won't be fulfilled until we know the love of God. How can we know the love of God if we don't trust Him? And how can we trust God if we can't trust our natural father?

It took me years to understand that God isn't like man. My view was damaged at the young age of five when Satan sent destructive assignments to mess up my life through my dad committing suicide.

So many women never get naked before God because they're fearful. They don't trust Him. They believe He's going to do to them what other people have done to them. But God is not a man that He should lie (see Numbers 23:19). God is faithful, and we'll find out that He is true. He will be there to the very end. He is full of grace and mercy. God is love, and He'll never leave nor forsake us.

He's not out to get you either. If God were after you, He would have caught you by now. Come on, He's God. The breath from His nostrils could destroy the whole nation. He already judged you when He hung Jesus on the cross. He justified you through the blood of Jesus Christ so you could be made whole. You are sanctified, justified, and chosen by the most high God.

> IF GOD WERE AFTER YOU, HE WOULD HAVE CAUGHT YOU BY NOW. COME ON, HE'S GOD.

LIFE LESSONS FROM LEAH

Genesis 29 tells the story of how Isaac sent his son Jacob back to his people to find a wife from among his wife's family. Rebekah, Isaac's wife, had a brother named Laban, who had two daughters, Leah and Rachel. Laban and Jacob struck a deal that if Jacob worked for Laban for seven years, Jacob could marry the shapely and beautiful Rachel. Apparently Leah was a "plain Jane," but Rachel was a knockout! Remember, men are sight-oriented.

Anyway, Jacob ended up married to Leah first as a result of Laban's deception. Many of us have been involved in relationships that have been conceived in deception. Honey, if it's a lie at noontime, it will be a lie at midnight. If it's a lie at midnight, it will be a lie in the morning. Anything birthed in deception will produce deception.

Now, Jacob didn't love Leah, and she was a woman (like all women everywhere) who desired to be loved. She craved affection. So she started having children, thinking if she produced sons for Jacob, he would love her. She had a son named Reuben, meaning "God has noticed my trouble." She had a second child whom she named Simeon, meaning, "Jehovah heard." Leah named her third son Levi, which means "attachment or to be joined to."

We want our husbands to notice us. Leah's names for her sons tell me that Jacob didn't even notice when Leah walked by (Reuben). He didn't think what she had to say was important (Simeon). When you're constantly ignored, it will mess with your mind because you begin to think, "Well, if people can discard me so easily, maybe I really don't have value. Perhaps I'm not important." And in naming her third boy Levi, it tells me that you can live in the same house and not be joined with someone. You can have a marriage license and a ring and not be joined. It says that just because you share the same bed doesn't mean you share intimacy.

Leah finally wised up. She finally said, "I'm not going to spend a lifetime trying to get you to look at me, listen to me, like me, and be intimate with me." She shifted gears. When people continually ignore you and don't notice and appreciate you, it's time to shift gears.

Leah's fourth son was named Judah, which means, "let Jehovah be praised." She was saying, "You go on about your life, Jake, but I'm not going to waste mine trying to get you to discern my values. You don't deserve my presence, and I'm not willing to spend my life trying to convince some fool that I'm worthy and valuable.

"God already told me that I am wonderfully and fearfully made. He created me unto good works. I'm going where I'll be celebrated."

We women do these kinds of things. We go on diets, thinking Mr. Right will pay attention to us if we're thin. Don't even try and act like you have never done such a thing. You know it's true!

You need to take care of yourself because you want to take care of yourself—not to attract someone's attention. Go back to school and get your education to equip yourself—not to impress someone. When you live your life for someone else, you're living in a fantasy that's going to crumble and come down hard on you.

You had better know who you are and live it out, because God has somebody for you who's not going to *compete* with you—he's going to *complete* you. You're not going to have to beg for his attention and cry for his love. He's going to celebrate and love you for who you are!

Stop trying to force-feed people who don't want you to feed them. There's a world out there that is dying, hungry, and thirsty for what God has deposited in you! Go to the multitudes that are starving!

RELINQUISHING UNHEALTHY ATTACHMENTS: ASSETS VS. LIABILITIES

In developing healthy relationships, you have to be able to recognize those that are toxic and walk away from them. Remember, you can't conquer what you won't confront, and you can't confront what you don't identify. I always say God uses people to bless you, and Satan uses people to mess you.

God did not create relationships to be a constant headache and hindrance in your life. A liability relationship can be defined as one that creates constant disagreement and strife. It will drain your energy. Where your energies are directed determines focus, and focus determines mastery, because whatever has the ability to keep your focus has mastered you.

If you're in a relationship that is draining the life out of you, you will not be effective on the job, in church, or in school. If you have to be this for him or that for her in order to maintain the relationship, something is wrong.

I've met women who work out sixteen hours a day because they're so afraid their man is going to see a better body than theirs. They become obsessed. It's not worth it. That relationship is a liability to you, and

. . . WHATEVER HAS THE ABILITY TO KEEP YOUR FOCUS HAS MASTERED YOU.

there are too many people who are going to love you, like you, and multiply your life—not divide it. Mark it a liability. "You're out!" You know, "One, two, three strikes and you're out at the old ball game!"

You can give them one or two chances to shape up, but three strikes, and it's time to say, "Baby, I'm out of here. You're messing me up, and you're not worth what I've been going through to keep you interested."

Another liability relationship is one that continually connects or ties you to your past. Look with me at the Word of God:

> *And when he was come into his own country, he taught them in their synagogue, insomuch that they were astonished, and said, Whence hath this man this wisdom, and these mighty works? Is not this the carpenter's son? is not his mother called Mary? and his brethren, James, and Joses, and Simon, and Judas? And his sisters, are they not all with us? Whence then hath this man all these things? And they were offended in him. But Jesus said unto them,*

A prophet is not without honour, save in his own country,
and in his own house. And he did not many mighty works
there because of their unbelief.

—MATTHEW 13:54-58

Jesus was able to do a few miracles in His hometown, but not as many as in other places, because the folks at home couldn't get past the fact that He was one of them—plain, ordinary, uneducated, small-town people. They couldn't receive from Him because they couldn't perceive who He was.

Perhaps those kinds of words have been spoken over you or someone you know. "Isn't that the girl who came out of the trailer park? Didn't she used to live in College Hill? Who does she think she is? Does she have a degree? Hasn't she been married and divorced twice?" People who hold you to your past are a liability in your life.

Philippians 3:13,14 tells us to forget those things that are behind and press toward the mark for the prize of the high calling. Move on . . . move ahead. Don't stay back there.

I'm not saying a common past is all bad. It unites your yesterdays, but common goals are much better because they unite your tomorrows. When you really think about it, there are very few people who can really grow with you. There are few people who can discern the gifts in you, love and appreciate you, and have the ability to handle you over there.

Few people are willing to go where God is taking you. Begin to accept it. Certain relationships are not worth hanging on to. Turn loose of those "friendships" that remind you of who you were, what you did, where you've been, where you came from, who your mama and daddy were, and move ahead with God. He has greater things for you.

I'm constantly taking inventory of relationships. How do you sort this through? I'll tell you:

1. Identify and accept the reality of the relationship. Admit to yourself that certain relationships are not working and move on. You can't fix everybody's problem. Bill Wilson of Metro Ministries in Brooklyn, NY, said this—and I love it—"People change, but not much." Releasing someone does not mean they will not get better. It just means God is better-suited to handle their problems at this time than you are. Release them to the One who will never fail them—release them to God.

2. Don't try to be someone else's God. There's a difference between helping someone and carrying them. Your constant help may be a hindrance. You are not the Holy Spirit. Don't be an enabler.

3. Be comfortable with criticism. When you've done all you can but determine the relationship must end, accept the fact that the person is going to be unhappy, and they're going to talk about you. When you decide to end an unhealthy relationship, a victim-mentality-minded person has to find a scapegoat. Guess who it's going to be?

4. Walk in forgiveness. Hurting people hurt people, and when they are drowning, they will kick and scream because they're hurt.

5. Develop a budget for each level of your relationship. Determine how much you're willing to invest in each relationship you have. Jesus ministered to multitudes, He was close to seventy people, even closer to twelve, intimate with three, and only one was very dear to Him. Every relationship takes a different investment. You have to budget.

In conclusion, I share this story. Years ago when we first started the church, somebody came to me who wanted to be my best friend. The truth is I'm too busy for a best friend. That may sound harsh, but I have a husband that I love and adore, and he's my best friend. I'm raising a child, and I'm a pastor, so that pretty much occupies my time.

This woman wrote me letters, sent me flowers, and regularly called to ask me out to lunch or to invite me to go with her to the mall. She was very nice.

Finally I took her out, and I said, "Look, the problem here is not you. It's me. I'm a lousy friend. I'm never going to call you or write to you. I'm not going to make the investment that will render the kind of return you're looking for, and you're going to be unhappy. The Bible says if you want to have a friend, you have to be one. I'm sorry, but I can't be your best friend."

Why would I do this? Because I've determined three things in my life. This probably wouldn't work for everybody, but it works for me. First and foremost, I want to hear God say, "Well done, thou good and faithful servant." Therefore, I'm going to fulfill the destiny that God has for me. In order to accomplish that, I have to stay very focused and disciplined and spend time in the Word of God.

Second, I'm going to be the best wife to Randy White that I can be. I'm going to stand before God and Randy White, and Randy is going to say that I was the best wife in the world. I will never deny him sexually. I will never tell him I have a headache. I will not come home and nag him. I'm going to take care of that man, and that man is going to be happy. He's going to walk around with a perpetual smile on his face and say, "Paula White is the light of my life." Why? Because I made a decision.

Third, I'm going to be the best mother to my child that I can be. I have a child. I am his mother until I die. So I will be the best mother I can be. I will nurture and protect him. No one else will be a better mother to him than I am.

You may think those aren't very many or noble goals for a person's life. There are only three, but they're big life goals. If I accomplish these three things, my life will have been successful. I will have made a difference.

I urge you to discern the relationships in your life. Develop healthy alliances that become assets . . . that multiply instead of divide you . . . that add without subtracting anything from you. You are in control of your life. You are the captain of your own vessel. Take control. God has good things for you!

DEVELOPING RELATIONSHIPS: LOVE WILL FIND A WAY

1. **Know and love yourself**
   a. The peace of knowing God is in control
   b. Confidence in God that passes all understanding
   c. You don't get intimate with God until you get naked

2. **Paul's thorn in the flesh**
   a. It keeps you on your knees
   b. There's a purpose for the storms in your life

3. **All of us want fulfillment**
   a. Where you won't find it: in money, job, position, house, car, etc.
   b. You were created for good works
   c. You're an ambassador on assignment
   d. You are who you are supposed to be

4. **Building on your differences**
   a. No cookie-cutter molds
   b. Be willing to do whatever it takes to reach others

5. **Mending damaged relationships**
   a. Relationships based on what we've been exposed to
   b. How we relate to others influences our perception of God

6. **Life lessons from Leah**
   a. Relationships birthed out of deception
   b. Improve yourself—but not to impress anyone but you
   c. God has deposited good things inside you

7. **Relinquishing unhealthy attachments**
   a. Recognize those that are toxic and walk away
   b. Define your liability relationships
   c. What you use to catch a mate is what it will take to keep him/her
   d. Take inventory of your relationships
      1. Accept the realities
      2. Don't try to be someone else's God
      3. Be comfortable with criticism
      4. Walk in forgiveness
      5. Develop a budget for each of your relationships

HOMEWORK ASSIGNMENT

Husbands and Wives

1. Meditate on Ephesians 3:13-20, asking God to plant the truth of these verses in your spirit man.

2. Ask God to help you to forgive everyone who ever hurt you, and release them to Him. Resist the temptation to allow any negative thought about these individuals to linger in your mind. If you have to, say aloud, "No, devil, I've forgiven them. I've thrown the memory of any wrongdoing into the sea of forgetfulness to be remembered no more."

3. Look in the mirror and thank God for you—how wonderfully He saw fit to make you. Then thank Him for your spouse, listing at least five attributes you most enjoy about him or her.

4. Realistically evaluate all of your relationships. Make a list of assets and liabilities. Pray for God to strengthen you in your inner man and help you to relinquish those associations that have kept you from growing mentally, spiritually, and emotionally.

Father, I love You. I thank You for the peace of knowing that You are in control of my relationships. Your Word says in 1 Peter 3:8 that I am to live in harmony with others, being sympathetic, loving, compassionate, and humble. I purpose in my heart to do that. Help me to be willing to do whatever it takes to make my marriage work. Give me wisdom, Lord, with regard to any unhealthy relationships that I've held onto. Keep me from saying hurtful things that wound others. I ask these things in Jesus' name. Amen.

FAMILY LIFE: STRIKING THE BALANCE

Randy: I know what it is to lose everything as a result of failing to realize the importance of balance in all things. I am convinced that God is concerned about every area of our lives, and I'm also sure He carefully watches to see exactly where we place our priorities. If family life is treated casually—just tucked into your schedule *if* you have the time—your life is out of balance and failure is a certainty, not a possibility.

I was brought up in a Christian home. In fact, my father was a full-gospel pastor. I was around the age of thirteen when I started to get involved in the ministry of my dad's church. I went on prison ministry trips, worked in the church's coffeehouse, and I even preached on the streets and in the parks occasionally.

In spite of all this, there was a period of restlessness during my teenage years that sometimes turned into a rebellious attitude toward God and my parents. I got so tired of hearing things like "You can't do that!" or "We don't believe in that!" I couldn't go swimming, bowling, or to the movies. I wasn't allowed to attend my high school prom. Sometimes it felt as though all our church knew was what we didn't believe in! Though I treasured my personal relationship with the Lord, I decided to find a way out from under all this religious legalism.

So when I met a nice girl, we got married. I was only seventeen! I had just graduated from high school, and we immediately left all that was familiar for Lee College, where I had enrolled as a student. I thought I knew quite a bit about the ministry and had some talent for Christian service. I was supremely confident that I had all the answers, and by getting married, I felt that I had found a way to be out from under the direction of my family and my church. I was on my own!

I truly loved the Lord and the work of the church. Quite honestly, I had never even considered any profession other than becoming a gospel preacher like my father. My wife, however, had little appreciation for my zeal and passion for ministry because she had no church background. We started a family after college, but we steadily grew further and further apart as I became successful in ministry.

My wife was a devoted mother to our three wonderful children, Kristin, Angie, and Brandon. Our children were her priority, while mine almost exclusively focused on my ministry activities. There was no balance in my life. I spent little time with my wife, and I really believed at the time that it was her job to handle everything at home while accommodating all of my plans and schedule. It was grossly unfair to her.

The better things went for me in ministry, the more my marriage and family suffered. I traveled a great deal as an evangelist, so I was gone most of the time. With three small children to take care of, my wife couldn't travel with me, so I failed to include her in my world. I had the mistaken notion that God would take care of my family since I was spending all my time working for Him.

By the time I realized how seriously our marriage had deteriorated, I didn't know how to disentangle myself from all the commitments on my time. We were in serious trouble. I had neglected my responsibilities as the head of my household by allowing the politics and mechanics of ministry to take precedence over my relationship with God. I believe when Christians experience failure, it is because of what they choose to do instead of following God's agenda for their lives.

Eventually my wife gave up on the marriage. I, too, was miserable. We separated, and with the realization that our differences truly were irreconcilable, we were finally divorced.

I no longer could be the associate pastor of the great church where my senior pastor was "grooming me to take over." I was no longer welcomed as an evangelist in all the churches across the nation where I had previously been scheduled. After all, I couldn't go and minister to others when my own life was out of order. In fact, because I was divorced, there was no place in my church association where I could officially function in any position of authority.

Within a matter of weeks following the divorce, I had lost everything. I could fit all that I owned into the trunk of my old '66 Mustang. After doing all I could to make sure that my wife and children were taken care of, I moved in with my parents, wondering if my life was over.

My priorities have radically changed since those days. Now my relationship to God, to Paula, and to my family always come before activities and things. But not then. I had to take a serious look at my priorities. Although I was involved in a variety of worthy ministry activities, my family only got what was left over . . . if I had anything left to give them at all.

GOD FIRST, YOU SECOND, FAMILY THIRD, JOB LAST

Paula: Let's look at Epaphroditus, a Christian believer from Philippi, who was sent to minister to the apostle Paul while he was imprisoned in Rome. Paul first mentions him in Philippians 2:25-30. The Bible says he worked himself in ministry to the point of death. Although Paul referred to this faithful messenger in glowing terms as his brother, companion, fellow worker, and fellow soldier, Paul also emphasized the importance of balance in 1 Corinthians 9:27 when he said, . . . *I keep under my body, and bring it into subjection: lest that by any means, when I have preached to others, I myself should be a castaway.*

So there's this thing called balance. We've heard about it a lot in the last decade or so, but what does it mean? Webster's dictionary defines *balance* as "emotional stability; a harmonious or satisfying arrangement of parts or elements; a force or influence tending to produce equilibrium; to bring into or maintain in a state of equilibrium."

It is important for us to understand that what is balanced for some people may not apply to you and your situation. The things that represent balance for Randy and Paula may not work for you. I'm a night person, for example. Your husband may be a day person. You may be content to stay at home while your mate is more comfortable being on the go.

I simply could not stay at home all the time. That is not my assignment in life. Randy and I would be in trouble if I were at home much more than I am, believe me! Our personalities, make-up, the call of God on our lives—all of these comprise how we function as we prioritize our lives.

Everybody isn't called to live in a Cape Cod-style Ozzie and Harriet house with a white picket fence and work from 9 to 5. A couple in our church, for example, has a very different lifestyle because of his career as a professional baseball player. God has anointed and blessed them to be on the road nine months out of the year while he plays ball. Now, how many women could go on the road nine months out of the year and live with that kind of schedule? God gives them grace for their call and their assignment.

Randy: **When Paula and I begin to feel a little tension between us, I'll say, "Go preach somewhere, honey." It brings balance into our lives for us to spend some time apart. You know, sometimes you can have a little too much of a good thing.**

Balance means to bring equality into all areas of our lives—not too much and not just barely enough, but equal parts. Our priority on our family must be the same as God's priority. Why? Because our relationship with our family illustrates our relationship with God.

Paula: Some husbands could not take their wife being gone sometimes seven to ten days a month, traveling and preaching. I'm home double the amount of time that I'm away. Our lives are well-balanced. My family definitely comes before my work.

STRIVE FOR BALANCE IN EVERY AREA OF YOUR FAMILY LIFE.

I recently read an interesting statistic: it's a proven fact that executives who value their families more than their businesses have their priorities in correct order. The executives are far more productive, creative, relaxed, and confident. I agree!

Randy: There has to be a lot of cooperation for a family to be successful. Dad, Mom, and the kids have to care for, love, and respect each other. That doesn't mean anyone has to walk around on eggshells—it means you can be yourself while you consider one another's needs.

Many people will speak into the life of your family—preachers, teachers, friends, and relatives. God often uses all of these important people to help you make a success of your marriage and family. Mutual trust, respect, loyalty, and forgiveness are enormous contributors to the success of any family. Without these, strife and chaos thrive and result in debilitating dysfunction.

For a family relationship to work, it's important to avoid bringing up past failures every time you get involved in a discussion. Even if you've been deeply wounded by a family member, you are not obliged to remind them of their transgressions for the rest of their lives. I know they've hurt you, but you need to grow up, pull yourself up by the bootstraps, and learn to forgive. Put it behind you.

You might say, "Well, I have a bad temper. Sometimes things just come up." There is nothing wrong with a temper—you can be angry and sin not. But when you repeatedly bring up the past, rehearsing old wounds like the lyrics to a song, you've crossed the line. Let it go!

Isaiah 43:18,19 says, *Remember ye not the former things, neither consider the things of old. Behold, I will do a new thing; now it shall spring forth; shall ye not know it? I will even make a way in the wilderness, and rivers in the desert.* And Philippians 3:13 says we are to forget those things that are behind us and press on.

There can be no balance in your life until you let go of old wounds. You ask, "What does that have to do with living a balanced life?" If you're thinking about the past all the time—how much you've been hurt—you won't move on and live in the now, let alone the future. Fear will paralyze your potential to trust in others to the point of affecting your ability to establish healthy relationships.

LOVE, CARE FOR, PROTECT, AND EXPECT

The Bible instructs husbands to love, care for, and protect their wives and children. They are *required* to provide the spiritual leadership of the home. Godly men lead by example. The "do as I say, not as I do" mentality has never worked, and it never will. Children should never be placed in a position where they can overhear their parents criticizing each other, and parents should never, ever take a child aside to confide their spouse's weaknesses and failures. This type of behavior is out of order, and God won't honor it.

Paula: When God created Eve for Adam, he really didn't realize anything was missing. He didn't know he was being groomed to be the head of a family. But when God caused Adam to go into a deep sleep and pulled Eve out of him, the Bible says it was so Adam would have a help meet—not a help mate as so many people say. Do you know what this tells me? It tells me that what Adam needed was already within him. It took God to pull it out of him.

It also meant companionship for Adam. Eve was to be his equal. He was not created to be superior to Eve. God simply made them to be similar . . . but different. The woman was given internal equipment the man didn't have—a womb in which to carry and nurture children until birth and mammary glands with which to nourish them after they were born. God prepared Eve to be a mother.

Randy: God set the man over the family. Again, the wife is to submit to the leadership of her husband, the husband is to love, honor, and cherish his wife, and the children are to obey their parents. Anything other than that is out of order.

When it comes to disciplining the children, I think it's important for kids to have a reverential fear of their parents.

The term *reverential fear* is not to imply that intimidating fear reigns in the household. To me, it means a healthy respect, and respect is earned, parents. It is not something you can dictate. *You will respect me because I am your father (or mother).* Discipline is born out of love, not pain and anger. And correction is merely loving direction. As we've said before, it doesn't involve the types of abuse we read about in the newspapers or see on TV talk shows.

The book of Proverbs begins by implying that all children are born in need of correction. It's not difficult to see that we never have to teach our children how to misbehave—they're born with a bent toward doing the wrong things. Parents are expected to lovingly but firmly train children in the ways of wisdom, responsibility, and righteousness. The direction children receive in the home sets the course for their entire lives according to Proverbs 22:6. Kids cannot rule the household.

Disciplining children has become a controversial subject, but it needn't be. Parents must be free to express displeasure at their child's unruly behavior in a godly fashion. I've said it before, and I'll say it again, I was spanked by both of my parents, and I have spanked my children. Parents who only threaten and don't follow through on their promises to have a "come to Jesus" meeting with their kids will lose the respect of their children.

Children who fail to learn that their inappropriate behavior carries consequences will eventually come to even more grief.

Parenting, whether proper or improper, shapes a child's future. We have so few opportunities to get it right that we must take it very seriously. It is critical to the success of your family that you set a godly example. Children need to see God in their mom and dad. Children who are taken to church sporadically learn to assume that the Lord isn't important unless it's convenient. This opens them up to all manner of compromises.

One successful pastor I know is the father of five adult children. He and his wife describe their family as a tiny nation with legislative, judicial, and executive branches and duties. When the children were young and still at home, their dad and mom were the king and queen, sons were princes, and daughters were princesses. These children were taught to be ambassadors-at-large for the family. Wherever they went, they were encouraged to be on their best behavior as representatives of their "country."

PARENTING, WHETHER PROPER OR IMPROPER, SHAPES A CHILD'S FUTURE.

These children are all grown up now and serving the Lord in a variety of ways. Expectations of them were high. They treated their parents with dignity and respect, and they were treated with equal respect and dignity. All five conformed to their parents' expectations of them.

Why do we treat our family members as second-class citizens and put on our "everything is wonderful" face in the church parking lot, greeting even the parking attendant with more respect than we display to those closest to us?

A recent *USA Today* article talked about the disrespect we see in America's teenagers toward their parents. The article defines the "helicopter" parent who hovers over the child and drives the child crazy with overprotective care and concern . . . and the angry parent who is devastated by his child's unruly attitude and tries to control the child with anger.

How do you deal with kids who seem to be coming along fine until they hit puberty and then suddenly are no longer recognizable because they've become so nasty and disagreeable? Take a long, hard look in the mirror. How was your behavior toward your parents as a teenager? I've found that when my kids act up, the very thing that I want to spank out of them is the thing I most dislike in myself.

The call and responsibility of parents are great, but beneath the title, "Parents," are just a man and a woman striving to be a success at one of the most important jobs in the world. Occasionally your child may need to see the real you. Your children may need help to understand that you are doing your best to try to facilitate and fulfill the role you've been given as a parent.

The Bible teaches that the man is the head of the house and the priest of his family. He is the spiritual leader—the one who determines the image of God that comes into the minds of children when they call Him "heavenly Father." You will never regret investing time in providing spiritual guidance for your family.

ON BEING SINGLE: SEEK GOD'S WILL AND NOT A SPOUSE

Paula: We have established that marriage is a divine institution ordained by God. For those who are single, though, it can be a time of frustration and frenzy. As surprising as it may be, the

Word of God has quite a bit to say on the subject of dating, courtship, and finding your mate.

Whether you are one who keeps trying and getting the same package (just wrapped differently), or one who has yet to find the perfect mate package with your name on it, we're going to be very frank about the single life and the hunt for Mr. and Ms. Right.

Perhaps you are one who keeps searching for tall, dark, and handsome, without realizing that his background and experience have equipped him to commit adultery on you five years down the road or to regularly use your body for a punching bag. Stop looking at the outside (the packaging) as you always have! Good looks don't come with a warranty for success and happiness!

This is how you're going to find your mate: *Delight yourself also in the Lord, and He will give you the desires and secret petitions of your heart* (Psalm 37:4 AMP). You have to start by working on your desires. When you delight in God, He's going to make your desires pure. He knows what you need much better than you do.

I'll use myself to illustrate my point. I never would have gone for a long-haired blonde, blue-eyed guy. I went for those dark-skinned guys. But God knew I needed Randy White. No one else could have tamed me or kept me under control. And God gave me Randy White. Hallelujah!

God knows exactly what you need, and He'll bring it to you if you will be patient and delight yourself in Him. Whether or not it seems you've waited for a long time, it doesn't take God years and years to get someone to you. He can change your life around in an instant. He can take you from the pit to the palace in twenty-four hours! He may bring your mate into your life today if you are sufficiently prepared to receive him or her.

Matthew 6:33 is such an important scripture in addressing

the issue of singleness. It tells us to . . . *seek ye first the kingdom of God, and his righteousness; and all these things shall be added unto you.* You have to stop seeking a person—stop seeking the idea of the person you want as a mate—and seek God. He has the perfect companion for you. And, as a side note, you aren't going to find your mate at Joe's Pool Hall, so stop trying to seek him or her there.

Some single folks go to church on Sunday, after spending Friday and Saturday nights in places where I can guarantee you God has not stashed your mate! You can be on the prowl for Mr. or Ms. Hot, but bars and clubs are where they're not! The Word is very clear about the perils of being unequally yoked:

> GOD CAN TAKE YOU FROM THE PIT TO THE PALACE IN TWENTY-FOUR HOURS.

> *Do not be unequally yoked with unbelievers [do not make mismated alliances with them or come under a different yoke with them, inconsistent with your faith]. For what partnership have right living and right standing with God with iniquity and lawlessness? Or how can light have fellowship with darkness?*
> —2 CORINTHIANS 6:14 AMP

Don't be anxious about being married. Why? Divorce statistics confirm that more than half of all married people are miserably unhappy . . . to the point that they are willing to spend their hard-earned money to dissolve the arrangement. Then they find someone else and do it all over again. They can't believe they got into such a mess. How did it happen?

That's not so difficult to figure out. God specifically instructed in His Word that Christians are not to even date unbelievers. Christians have no business going out with someone who is not born again and filled with the Spirit of God. If you are, you need to cut that relationship off today! And you can take this statement to the bank: **There should be no such thing as premarital sex.** It is ungodly, and it will send your soul to hell. If you take fire into your bosom, you're going to be burned (see Proverbs 6:27). I don't care what type of sex it is—it is wrong outside of marriage.

Randy: **You don't want a spouse if it isn't God's will for you. First Corinthians 7:1 deals with actually choosing a spouse, temptation, and marriage. We'll read the Amplified version,** *Now as to the matters of which you wrote me. It is well [and by that I mean advantageous, expedient, profitable, and wholesome] for a man not to touch a woman [to cohabit with her] but to remain unmarried.* **That word** *cohabit* **with her means "to live together in a sexual relationship when not legally married." That's Webster's definition. My own definition of the word is "to shack up."**

Verse 2 in the King James Version says, *Nevertheless, to avoid fornication, let every man have his own wife, and let every woman have her own husband.* **In other words, if that drive inside of you is so strong that you think you're going to compromise, you had better do whatever it takes to bring your flesh under subjection to the Holy Spirit or find your life partner.**

Why would Paul say it was good for a man to avoid marriage? I've read several different explanations. Some say it is Paul's response to a problem in the Corinthian church

referred to in verse 26, *I suppose therefore that this is good for the present distress.* . . . Others think Paul's opponents may have said it to discredit him.

Still others think it refers to verses 12-16 of chapter 6, indicating that some Christians in the church at Corinth thought so highly of themselves spiritually that they could do whatever they wanted to with their bodies while others were so spiritual that they maintained they were "above" indulging in sexual intercourse even in marriage.

I believe verses 32-35 of chapter 7 state the real reason Paul brought it up at all. The unmarried can devote all their time directly to the Lord. Those who are married have to focus on their marriages.

Paula: Don't get us wrong—when God is in a relationship, you know it. If you're a committed Christian, you'll also know it when God isn't involved. That girl or guy may look fabulous on the outside, but if they're full of vinegar on the inside, any happiness you thought you'd found with this person will quickly subside.

> IT TAKES MORE THAN GOOD LOOKS AND A FINE BODY TO MAKE IT IN THIS MARRIAGE DEAL!

I know I've said this before, but when Randy and I were called to Tampa from Washington, D.C., we didn't know how much faith it would take for us to recover financially and get back on our feet. If a pee-stained mattress is your idea of living the high life, you might be all right. If you're okay with having to believe God for food for your child, that's great. But we were able to stick it out through thick and thin because of the strong anointing of God on our lives for what He'd called us to do, in addition to the love *He* had placed in each of us for the other.

There had to be more than good looks and a fine body to bring us to the finish line in this marriage deal. As I've said, trouble is no respecter of persons. It will find out where you live and set up housekeeping.

This principle we've previously discussed of putting God first in your life also applies to singles who are involved in a relationship with an unbeliever. Stop thinking you're going to win your unsaved potential spouse to the Lord. A leopard cannot change his spots (see Jeremiah 13:23). People cannot change other people. It's difficult enough for the Spirit of God to change a person. At least, if you have a Christian vessel, you can go to his or her supervisor, the Holy Spirit, and ask Him to deal with that person. If he or she isn't even a Christian, even that hope is considerably diminished.

Some people spend all their prayer time loosing and binding, and they don't even have anything yet. The key to finding your mate is in first seeking God. Set aside your glorious expectations—you know, those dreams that everything is going to be all right when you get married. Guess what? *Everything* won't be all right.

Marriage is not a solution to any of your problems. Instead, whatever problems you've had will be compounded many times. Couples that constantly fight while dating are going to fight constantly after they get married. Amos 3:3 says, *Can two walk together, except they be agreed?* You can't walk together if you are in constant disagreement. And James 3:16 says, *For where envying and strife is, there is confusion and every evil work.* The Greek word for *confusion* means "instability and a state of disorder." James 1:8 says, *A double minded man is unstable in all his ways.*

Don't even think that an unstable, confusing, strife-filled relationship with someone isn't going to affect you, because it will. It will affect the way you feel about yourself, how you produce on your job, how you mother your children, how you carry out the business of the kingdom of God, and literally every other thing in your life. Living in an unstable state of confusion is not God's will for any believer, so if strife and constant disagreement are identifiable liabilities in a relationship you're currently involved in, don't even hesitate to cut it off. The relationship is not worth anything to you. It is a liability and isn't likely to ever fall into the asset column.

Finally, please don't think having a child is going to solve anything. This seems to be an idea that women come up with far more often than men. Ladies, if you think bringing a baby into your mess will keep him from stopping at the bar on his way home from work and spending his paycheck, you're mistaken. If you think a tiny, little, innocent infant will motivate him to go to church with you every week, you are setting yourself up for disappointment.

Take an inventory of your relationships, single man or woman of God. Sort through and relinquish the unhealthy ones that diminish you in any way. Fantasyland already has too many residents. You know who you are. You still bring out your *Pretty Woman* videotape and think some Richard Gere is going to come pick you up off your street corner and sweep you off your feet.

You cling to the knight-in-shining-armor mentality that says, "someday your prince will come." Honey, ride your own horse. Be your own knight in shining armor. You don't need anybody to come along and make your dreams come true. You had better identify the reality of your relationship before you get married. If you don't, when the honeymoon is over, you're going to find that his feet stink. He has bad breath when he wakes up in the morning. He probably won't pick up his clothes or hang up the wet towels after he takes a shower.

And you guys need to realize before you say "I do" that she's probably not going to go to the ballgame with you on Friday nights like she does now to impress you. If you're shopping with her on Saturday afternoon to keep her happy while you're dating instead of sitting at home in your sweats and watching the game, that's what you're going to be doing after the rice has been thrown. She most likely won't want to stay home on Saturday night and watch action movies with you as she's doing now and telling you what a great time she's having. She's going to want to be taken out for dinner and a romantic movie. Bubba, you've been deceived!

All relationships take work. Admit to yourself when a relationship isn't working, identify the problems, even discuss them if you can, but don't let your emotions disguise the obvious realities. Time is limited. It is the most precious and valuable gift that God has given you. It's your greatest commodity. Invest it wisely in alliances that will render a healthy return. Recognize when your efforts to rehabilitate a person have failed and move on.

As a pastor, this subject of evaluating relationships is a difficult one because I want to help everybody. I want to be there for everyone. And I want to fix everybody's problems. I had to get real with myself and recognize there were some relationships that were draining me and keeping me from God's real purpose for my life.

While I was sitting in counseling sessions with people and repeating for the second and third time what I had told them the first time we met, my time and God's purpose for my life were being stolen. How often did I need to repeat the same counsel? How many times were we going to step on this same merry-go-round? If you're not going to make it work, then it's not going to work for you. You've become a deficit—not just to yourself—but also to me.

I've allowed my time to be taken from someone who really wanted and needed my counsel and was willing to receive it. And I neglected the time I should have spent alone with God and in prayer, preparing to minister to the masses.

Let's look again at Jeremiah 13:23 in The Amplified Bible, *Can the Ethiopian change his skin or the leopard his spots? Then also can you do good who are accustomed and taught [even trained] to do evil.* If you're black, can you turn to white today? And if you're white, can you turn to black? No way. You can't change the color of your skin. This is the Word of the Lord—this isn't Paula White. People change, but not much.

Releasing someone does not mean they will never get better—it just means God is better suited to handle their problems at this time than you are. Release them to the One who will never fail them—release them to God.

RUSHING INTO MARRIAGE—JUST SAY "NO!"

I think Bill Wilson from Metro Ministries in Brooklyn, NY most wisely describes the consequences of being impulsive when it comes to marriage. Bill lives in New York, the home of famous

Central Park. I'll try to put it as succinctly as Bill did when he spoke at Without Walls International Church. Bill said, "Picture a young couple in love sitting on a bench in beautiful Central Park. They're holding hands. It's about four o'clock in the afternoon, and the temperature is around 72 degrees. The wind is blowing. She is wearing her Chanel No. 5. She has on those high-heeled shoes that really accentuate her shapely legs. She looks like a million dollars. Her makeup is just right. She's perfect!

"Suddenly this young man lets his hormones take over, and he thinks, *I need to marry this wonderful woman!* So he gets down on his knees and asks, 'Will you marry me?' This is not the time to ask someone to marry you."

Bill said what that young man needs to do is wait until five o'clock the next morning, and then pay a surprise visit to her apartment. He should knock on the door and say, "Hello! I'm here!" Then he should walk in and see the condition of the apartment. He should take an inventory of how her hair looks when it's not blowing in the wind on a balmy 72-degree day in the park. He needs to observe how she looks *au naturel*—without any makeup.

I add to this that the same observations apply to the fellas. Ladies, take note of how he's groomed, look at the condition of his car, his clothes, and his shoes. Then visit his apartment. Is he neat? Does he keep things orderly? Or is he a slob who looks great when he's out on the town, but is in danger of hurting himself while trying to negotiate the walk from the foyer to the kitchen?

You may think that sounds mean and unfair. The truth is this is exactly what needs to happen. Take the blinders off and see things as they are—not how you'd like for them to be. Marriage has never solved a problem that I can identify, with the possible exception of lust. You have to decide just how willing you are to satisfy your burning flesh.

If you can occupy yourself with activities that take your mind off of the desires of the flesh, focus on God and His plan, and trust Him to bring your life partner to you in His perfect timing, you'll spend the rest of your lives together being grateful for the fruit of patience and the gift of wisdom.

If you're seriously thinking about marrying someone who promises that he or she is going to get saved, come to church with you, and raise your children in a godly home, I still advise you to wait until you see him or her saved and in church for a long time. I'll go even further—if he's making $3 million a week and can't tell you enough how much he loves you, don't get married unless and until you honestly believe in your heart that your relationship is based on the Lord Jesus Christ. Otherwise, it won't work. Christ is the only foundation on which you can build a godly life.

God has a good plan for your life. Jeremiah 29:11 AMP was written for you! *For I know the thoughts and plans that I have for you, says the Lord, thoughts and plans for welfare and peace and not for evil, to give you hope in your final outcome.*

FAMILY LIFE:
STRIKING THE BALANCE

1. **Randy's testimony of what an imbalanced life cost him**
   a. Epaphroditis "working himself to death" for the ministry
   b. Cooperation must reign in any successful family
   c. Avoid bringing up past failures

2. **Love, care for, protect, and expect**
   a. Husbands are to love, care for, and protect
   b. Wives are to honor, esteem, and admire
   c. Parenting (good or bad) shapes a child's future
   d. Example of a godly Christian preacher's home

3. **The single life: seek God's will and not a spouse**
   a. Stop looking at the outside package
   b. Delight in the Lord, and He'll give you your desires
   c. Take care with regard to where you're looking
   d. Avoid fornication
   e. Marriage is not the solution to any problem
   f. Having a child won't solve your problems either
   g. The "Knight in Shining Armor" syndrome—get over it!
   h. Test the waters. Look at his/her car, apartment, grooming
   i. Don't marry an unbeliever

Homework Assignment

Perform one of these tasks each week for a month:

1. Individually list and evaluate your priorities. Who is first in your life?
2. Write a plan of action for bringing balance into your relationship.
3. Think of ways you can overcome distractions in your marriage.
4. Write your spouse a love letter and hide it under his/her pillow.

*Father, in the name of Jesus, I commit myself to giving
You first place in my marriage and in my family. My
delight is in You, Lord. I follow after love and strive to live
in peace with everybody. Your Word declares that when I
keep my tongue free from evil and my lips from guile, I
will enjoy life and see good days. Thank You for the good
days I've already enjoyed and those that are still to come. I
believe and say that I walk in balance, wisely prioritizing
that which You have set before me to do. I make a
conscious effort to believe the best of my spouse, enduring
anything and everything that comes my way without
weakening. I praise You, Father, that You have enabled
me to train my children in the way they should go. Hear
my praise unto You, Lord, for Your goodness truly endures
forever. Amen.*

seven

STRENGTHENED THROUGH STRUGGLE

Paula: When God raises you up, you're raised up. When God promotes you, you're promoted. When God blesses you, you are blessed, and nobody can do anything about it. So when you're struggling—and everybody has a struggle to deal with at one time or another—you need to know that no one can pluck you out of the hand of God.

If you've somehow managed to obtain a copy of this "marriage manual," and you've read this far, you must be someone who wants to know how to turn a struggling marriage into a strong one. You may not like what I'm going to tell you, but I'm going to go ahead and tell you anyway, because this is one of the things you just may need to do. You may have to humble yourself.

"What? Pastor Paula, you've got to be kidding!" I know what you're thinking, but let's take a look at 1 Peter 5:6 AMP,

Therefore humble yourselves [demote, lower yourselves in your own estimation] under the mighty hand of God, that in due time He may exalt you.

If you've ever suffered from low self-esteem, you may think, *How could I possibly humble myself any more than I have already? I'm a grasshopper in my own eyes!* Or low self-esteem may cause you to exaggerate everything out of proportion as you attempt to make yourself and everything you do seem bigger and better in order for you to feel comfortable in your own skin.

Believe me, I'm taking you somewhere in this chapter, so stick with me. Peter's phrase *in due time* is very interesting. In the Greek it means *kyros,* or "a set or proper" time. In other words, if I am willing to humble myself or go through this process, then God himself will exalt me. I'm not talking about your spouse, your best friend, your boss, or your pastor exalting you. I'm talking about being exalted by God at a pre-set time.

Ecclesiastes says there is a time and season for everything (see Ecclesiastes 3:1). God created time. He has set an appointed time to raise you up. There's a time set for your marriage. There's a time set for the breakthrough your marriage needs. There's a time set for you! There's a set time for you to move from poverty to prosperity. There's a time set for you to stop fighting that devil you've fought for forty years.

There's a time for your marriage to be healed if it's wounded. There's a time for you and your spouse to be set free from the bondages that have wreaked havoc in your lives. If you'll remain humble before God, in due season (His set time), He will exalt you.

What happens if you are too impatient to wait for God's time? Can we say Ishmael? Genesis 16-25 describes the perils of impatience. Marriage contracts during that period of time provided for husbands to use slave-girls to bear children that would become the wife's in the event that she was childless. Sarai gave Abram her slave-girl, Hagar, in order to have a son. She named the child Ishmael, and the heartache that resulted produced a myriad of complex situations. Read it sometime.

When you are too impatient to wait for the promise of God, you will begin to work things out within your own flesh. When that happens, you often create a whole new set of problems. And you have to deal with Hagar and Ishmael for the rest of your natural life.

Remember when I said that whatever you do to get a mate you must continue doing to keep him? In the flesh, it may seem as though divorce court is an attractive option because the new guy at the office is looking pretty fine! You had better just hold on because your breakthrough is coming! Your husband (or wife) is about to start looking pretty good to you again.

Hebrews 6:12 tells us that the promises of God are inherited through our faith and patience—at a set time. That's why Psalm 1:1-3 says, *Blessed is the man that walketh not in the counsel of the ungodly, nor standeth in the way of sinners, nor sitteth in the seat of the scornful. But his delight is in the law of the Lord; and in his law doth he meditate day and night. And he shall be like a tree planted by the rivers of water, that bringeth forth his fruit in his season; his leaf also shall not wither; and whatsoever he doeth shall prosper.*

This blessed person does not sit around showing contempt for his or her spouse, seeking advice from unbelievers who don't have a clue as to what path to follow since they have no leading from the Holy Spirit. The blessed person has joy that comes from the Word of God. He eats the Word of God. He hungers and thirsts after it. He mentally images God's Word working on his behalf. He knows that the Word is a higher law than every natural law.

The individual who does this keeps his hands clean and his heart pure, knowing that his reward is about to come forth in God's season. So many couples get right to the edge of their breakthrough . . . then give up and give in because it feels like they've done everything they know to do and still nothing is happening. You must understand that sometimes God will let you circle the mountain again and again. He will let you keep going around and around.

He won't let you graduate until you've learned your lesson. Perhaps you have circled the mountain more times than you care to remember. I've done that myself in some areas of my life. At times it seems like all hell is breaking loose, but I must remind myself that my God is bigger and greater than any problem I've ever faced and that He will bring forth my fruit (reward) when He knows I'm ready to receive it.

This may mean you have to keep telling your husband how much you love him even when he's cussing you out. You may think he's been acting like a fool . . . dancing with the devil in the blue dress. But keep telling him, "You are the high priest of this household. You are God's righteousness." God has a set time to bring forth your reward, and when it comes, He will put a hook in your man's jaw as he sits on that Budweiser stool out at Joe's Pool Hall and bring him in. Whatever you do shall be profitable and shall break forth in the name of Jesus!

Just say to yourself right now, "I am being strengthened through my struggle."

YOU WON'T SEEK WHAT YOU'RE NOT DESPERATE FOR

Acts 13:22 AMP describes Israel's King David as a man after God's own heart . . . *who will do all My will and carry out My program fully.* God was close to David because David's heart was *in pursuit of* God. The only prerequisite to finding is seeking, and you won't seek what you are not desperate for. David was *desperate for* God. His life was not about mere existence, but about fulfilling the will of God.

You are much more than a bag of bones. You are more than a pretty little package in pigtails. You have a purpose and plan in the mind of Almighty God who fashioned and formed you and wonderfully and fearfully created you. You are an intricate piece in His puzzle. He raised you up for such a time as this. Genetically, you are perfect. Your race is perfect, your personality is perfect. And here's a flash: *so is your spouse's!*

You may be the loudmouth in your marriage, or you may be the quiet one. Whichever way it is, you were created by God to be who you are! Nobody else in all of eternity will ever be packaged exactly like you.

We spend a lifetime trying to be what we were not created to be. We want to be like everybody else. We need to stop that right now. Randy White did not marry me because I reminded him of all his other girlfriends. I did not marry Randy White because he reminded me of my old boyfriends. It is our differences that set us apart and give us value. We need to start enjoying our uniqueness. It equips us to fulfill the plan and purpose of God for our lives.

If someone can't see what's on the inside of you, don't waste your lifetime trying to convince them to love you. Esteem your differences—I am saying this to both husbands and wives . . . and to singles, for that matter.

David was chosen by God for special things, but his accomplishments didn't come without pain and heartache. In Psalm 61, we are allowed to look in on a private moment in David's life. Most people don't like for us to see them in their private moments. Guess what? You won't always have on your mascara, Miss Priss. And, Mr. Man, you won't always have a perfect haircut, shave, just the right shirt, slacks, and shoes when somebody's looking at you.

We're given a glimpse of David in a private moment when he cries out to God as he is faced with yet another traumatic blow from the forces of life. The Bible says it rains equally on the just and on the unjust (see Matthew 5:45). You would probably rather not hear that, but just knowing it can help to strengthen you in the midst of your struggle. You are not the only person who has ever had a problem. You are not alone!

You cannot simply pray all of your struggles away, because sooner or later God will make you look at the reality of them, and you'll be stronger for having faced them head on. Maintaining a happy marriage is a challenge. No one can honestly deny the knowledge that marriage requires hard work. There are times when something happens that can knock the breath out of you. There are times when you wonder, "What went wrong? How did we get here? Why are we facing this problem? I thought we had conquered these troubles when such and such happened. Yet here we are again, faced with yet another traumatic blow.

"God, I love You, and I'm serving You, but things aren't going like I thought they would. I know it's not You, God, but right now, I feel like I'll crumble under the pressure. My heart is overwhelmed, God. And just when I thought the bad dreams had ended, I find myself in this nightmare again."

Have you ever been there? Perhaps jealousy has come back to visit your house. Maybe it is insecurity. It could be financial problems. These issues tear at the heart of even the most solid Christian marriages and homes. Perhaps your child is out running around, drinking, smoking, drugging, or spending time with unsuitable "friends." Your spouse might be having an affair, or maybe you're having an affair. Your home is about to split completely apart. Times are tough. Are you tough enough to wait patiently for the Lord to deliver your breakthrough?

> MAINTAINING A HAPPY MARRIAGE IS A CHALLENGE . . . AND IT REQUIRES HARD WORK.

King David was in trouble. In Psalm 61:1-3 AMP, he says, *Hear my cry, O God; listen to my prayer. From the end of the earth will I cry to You, when my heart is overwhelmed and fainting; lead me to the rock that is higher than I [yes, a rock that is too high for me]. For You have been a shelter and a refuge for me, a strong tower against the adversary.*

I've said it before and I'll say it again—trouble is no respecter of persons. It is not prejudiced toward you. It doesn't care about your social or economic status. It doesn't care what color you are. It doesn't care about your husband's family. It doesn't care who your pastor is or what church you attend. It has no regard whatsoever for how many degrees you have or how important your job is.

Trouble will invade your life in the most unfair manner. It has no scruples . . . no ethics. It will come through your spouse, your parents, your children, your church brothers and sisters, and even through your pastor. It really doesn't give a rip what vessel it has to occupy as long as it can do one thing—leave your heart overwhelmed, hopeless, and helpless. It will leave you bleeding, broken, and hung out to dry.

Many theologians call Psalm 61 the supplication psalm. *Supplication* means to "beseech or implore; to ask or beg in a humble way to do something or give something." *Beseech* is a very strong word. It means, "He-e-e-e-e-y-y-y-y-y!" Psalm 61 is an SOS psalm. David is saying, "I'm in trouble. I'm anointed, chosen by God, but I'm in trouble. My heart is overwhelmed. I'm about to die inside here. All hell's breaking loose!"

So often we, in the church, are hypocritical. Just ask someone in the world. The world says, "The church is full of hypocrites!" And they're right! We aren't real in church. We wear our masks. We say, "Everything's great! We've got the victory! Praise the Lord! My marriage is terrific! My kids are on fire for God!" And we fuss and fight all the way to the church parking lot, saying awful things to each other and putting on quite a show for our children who will most likely follow in our footsteps because of the great example we gave them!

And struggle or trouble is not a one-time event. It's cyclical. It comes in cycles. Live long enough and you will find out that life is nothing but a series of cycles. Ecclesiastes 1:9 AMP says, *The thing that has been—it is what will be again, and that which has been done is that which will be done again; and there is nothing new under the sun.*

In other words, I can tell my future by looking at the past. I

know we don't like to hear it,
but history repeats itself—the
cities, names, and factors may
be different, but the storyline is
the same. Different church
folks, but the same mess. I've
discovered that you can't change the events of life. You can't even
"faith" them away.

It takes more faith to walk through the struggle than to be delivered from it. I can't stop things from happening, but I can change my attitude toward them. It really doesn't matter *what* you and I go through. What matters is *how* we go through it. How do we respond to it? How does it position us mentally? How do we feel about the cycle of life we're in?

In Ephesians 3:16, Paul prayed that we would be strengthened in the inner man. See, there was a storm. There was tribulation—a crisis of major proportions. Paul didn't pray storms away. He prayed to be strengthened as a result of the storm. Storms don't break us—they make us. We're becoming a stepping stone, not a stumbling block.

When you pray for your marriage situations and circumstances to go away, it's like putting a Band-Aid on a broken arm. The problem is not solved. But when you can adjust and change your attitude toward the problems, you will receive wholeness.

I hate to tell you this, but when you've conquered the situation you're facing right now, another one is going to come along. If you're going to survive, you have to change the way you respond to the challenges life throws at you. You can change the way you feel about your spouse. You can change your mind about your kids.

I lived in depression for years. One day I just decided that the joy of the Lord was going to be my strength. I changed my mind. I deliberately altered my thinking about the circumstances that were causing me to be depressed.

We can learn so much about life by reading the Bible—particularly as we look at David. We are able to see him as a young boy, the youngest of eight sons of Jesse. When the prophet Samuel came to Jesse's house to tell him God had chosen one of his sons to be king, Jesse lined up seven of his eight boys for the prophet to look at, not even considering David as a contestant. Jesse didn't give David a fighting chance. He appeared to see no value in David at all, completely disregarding the fact that God could ever use him.

And you see that pattern of rejection following David in 1 Samuel 17, as his brothers laughed and made fun of him when he came to the Israeli-Philistine battlefront to get a report on the war for his dad and to bring the older boys a sack lunch. David's brothers rejected him because their father did.

Perhaps rejection has followed you around from childhood. Your parents rejected you, so your siblings followed suit. Or you went to school, and classmates didn't include you in their activities. It doesn't matter. Man may have rejected David, but God's hand was on him. God had anointed David to be king, despite the fact that his family saw no good in him.

When people reject and disappoint you, it's difficult to feel good about yourself. It messes with your mind. You think if they're so willing to disregard you, you must not be very valuable. And you will never possess what God has promised because you don't see yourself as worthy or valuable. The devil assigns failure to all of us, but he is a liar!

David had to overcome a heritage of rejection. And the Bible says, in order to do all the will of the Lord, David had to convince himself that what others said to and about him simply was not true! It wasn't easy. David was vulnerable. He was looking for acceptance that was never given to him by a father who had rejected him.

First Samuel 16:21 says, *And David came to Saul, and stood before him: and he loved him greatly; and he became his armour-bearer.* Seeking acceptance and approval, David ran into the arms of a madman who absolutely tried to destroy him. He jumped from the frying pan into the fire! Cycles, cycles. A different name, but the same thing is going on. And this time, it's not just emotional trauma and a wounded soul. This time it's twenty-one attempts on his life! This time it's his mentor trying to murder him. This time it's life or death.

Continually faced with these traumas, David married Michal, Saul's daughter. She was part of his reward for killing Goliath. There will always be a reward in your life when you defeat your enemy (giant). She wasn't merely a booby prize. First Samuel 18:20 says Michal loved David greatly. When her mad, crazed father was hunting David down to kill him, Michal and David were separated, and she was given to a man by the name of Phalti.

When David was restored and began to rule over Judah, he made a covenant with Saul's former military commander, Abner, on the condition that Michal would be returned as his wife. He didn't need Michal. He was married to Abigail. He had other women—beautiful wives and concubines. Obviously, he had enough sex. But David loved Michal. Sadly, when she came back, David discovered that Michal had the same critical spirit that was on her daddy. She was the sad seed of a bitter, critical father who failed to walk with God.

Maybe you're looking in the mirror and hating what you see. You've always said, "I'll never be like my mother," but you find yourself driving your husband away because you're talking more and more like Mama. It's time to break that destructive habit in the name of Jesus. It's time to be loosed from that curse once and for all. Michal was so bitter that she resented David's happiness. If you don't deal with your bitterness, you'll drive everyone away from you.

Second Samuel 6:16 says when the Ark of the Covenant was returned to Jerusalem, King David danced before the Lord, and Michal despised him in her heart. Different name, different face, different place, but the same old story line: *rejection*. David was rejected by the one who should have valued him most. He was mocked by the wife who should have celebrated his success. First his father, then his brothers, then his mentor, now his wife. Later, even his own children would reject him.

YOU CAN'T MOVE FORWARD WHEN YOU'RE PARALYZED

Like David, we find ourselves desiring to do the will of God. But you can have that desire and still be filled with pain—pain that will make you lose heart. Pain that will desensitize you. Pain that will make you sit and wonder, "How did this happen to me? My husband (wife) doesn't love me. My kids are a mess. I try and try, and all I do is fail." Pain can be so paralyzing that it causes you to get stuck in one of those cycles of life.

Are you stuck? Are you stuck because of words that were spoken over you as a child? By a spouse? By your own child? Have you suffered the kind of pain that causes a woman to say, "I'll never trust another man again." Do you understand pain that can cause a man to be bitter toward all women because he couldn't get along with his mother? Does pain have you stuck?

You were destined by God for greatness, but if you're stuck in one of those cycles we've been talking about, you're in danger. Why? Because if you're ever going to possess what God has promised, you must keep moving forward. When you get stuck in one of the cycles of life, you tend to freeze and become paralyzed because the pain is so great. You can't move forward when you're paralyzed.

That's why Paul said in Philippians 3:13,14, . . . *forgetting those things which are behind, and reaching forth unto those things which are before, I press toward the mark for the prize of the high calling of God in Christ Jesus.* In spite of the painful circumstances that seem impossible, you sometimes have to let go and press on. In this context, *press* means "to resist that which would resist you." You think, "I've got to do something. I can't just sit down on this one. I've got to press on and forget those things that are behind me."

> . . . IF YOU'RE EVER GOING TO POSSESS WHAT GOD HAS PROMISED, YOU MUST KEEP MOVING FORWARD.

That may mean you have to forget that you were once a prom queen, admired and respected by your peers. Forget that you once made a million dollars but don't have it now. Forget that you were once happily married but aren't happy now. You must press forward. Press. Press. Press.

This is why Paul said in 2 Timothy 4:7 AMP, *I have fought the good (worthy, honorable, and noble) fight, I have finished the race, I have kept (firmly held) the faith.* Here's the problem: sometimes we won't press because we're too afraid or too tired to fight. The key to finishing your course is pressing on no matter what. It is fighting the good fight when you feel like giving up and quitting. It is pressing on when you're wondering, "How many times does my heart have to be ripped out?"

Keeping the faith means keeping on even when you're thinking, "I thought when I married him that he would never walk out on me, but my nightmare is back." Fighting the good fight means going on even though you thought when you finally forgave the people who tied you up in a closet and abused your little body that nobody would ever hurt you again. And yet, here you are.

Granted, it's easier to give up. You may feel like saying, "God, I'm just plain tired of fighting. I'm tired of trying to possess what You have promised. I just want to sit here and rest. Is there anybody out there who will be true to me? Is there anybody that won't hurt me? Is there any cycle of life that won't bring me back to this same place? I've fought and I've fought. I'm too tired to keep fighting."

But you must not give up. You must get back up one more time. Keep the faith—run one more lap. Once you have a word from God that you can stand on—a word that says your marriage and family are going to work no matter how bad it looks now— be prepared for all hell to break loose in your life, because it will. The enemy of your soul has an assignment with your name on it. The harder you press in to possess God's promise, the more the enemy will try to target you for destruction because he wants to kill the Word inside of you.

CRY OUT TO GOD

Whose report will you believe? You have to believe what God says. Stand upon the higher law right now. Let them repossess your house and your car. This isn't the end of the story. So what if your wife comes home one night and says, "I want a divorce. I've been having an affair with a guy at the office, and I'm leaving." You have a word from the Lord. This isn't the last chapter. Keeping the faith means keeping up the good fight.

I wish I could say to everybody who reads this book, "You're going to make it!" But to make it, you're going to have to fight. You're gaining strength as you struggle! The greater the problem, the more you'll move toward God. Begin to cry out as David did, "Hear my cry!" The Hebrew word for cry is *rhina*. It means "a shrill sound." There are some things that leave you so broken, so busted, so messed up, that you can't articulate them without screaming.

You may not be comfortable with my transparency, but there are some things in my life that have hurt me so badly that I couldn't even explain them to you. All I could do was cry out. There are some things that have pierced my heart so deeply that they have taken my breath away. I was so disappointed that I couldn't even pray for any specific thing. All I could do was cry out, "Hear me, my God. Oh, God, hear my cry!" The words, "Oh, God" translate to *elohim* in Hebrew. *Elohim* means "a righteous judge." Romans 12:19 AMP says, . . . *Vengeance is Mine, I will repay (requite), says the Lord.*

There are three things you can't touch in the Word of God. You can't touch His glory, you can't touch the tithe, and you can't touch vengeance. God says, "I'll make every wrong right. I'll make every crooked path straight. I am a righteous judge. Vengeance is for Me to take care of—not for you to bother yourself with."

Like the woman with the issue of blood (see Matthew 9:20), you have to press in. God knows what issues you're dealing with right this minute. He knows what you're suffering from. He knows what you're dying from. He knows. He touched me and attended to my prayer, and He'll do the same for you.

You may be thinking, "My husband loves me, but my children and I are having a falling out. It's breaking my heart." Someone else may think, "My husband's acting like a fool. What's the matter with him? What's wrong with me that he would go out and run around on me?" Another may be thinking, "I've just lost my job. Why can't I get along with my boss? Oh, God, what am I to do?"

Where can you go for help? David asked God to attend unto his prayer from the end of the earth . . . from his wilderness place he would cry out to God.

Genesis 49 says it is the hand of the Lord that delivers us. Only God can uphold you and attend to your prayer. God is going to pick you up from your place of brokenness when your heart is overwhelmed. He will transport you to the rock or refuge that is higher than you. God is higher than your situation. He is higher than your heartache. He is higher than your hurt and pain. He will elevate you above it all. You may be in deep trouble, but you're not going to be affected by it.

There is a strong tower where you can run for safety and shelter from the enemy—you can make it through that cycle that seeks to destroy you, your marriage, your children, your relationships, your health, your wealth, and your intimate walk with God. Your situation may not change, but you can change. Your circumstances don't have to affect you.

Your husband or wife may walk through the door of the room where you sit right now, reading this book. He may be cursing like a sailor, but you can have a new love for your mate when you choose to see him as God sees him. Wife, see your husband as the high priest of your household. Husband, look at the wife of your youth as King Solomon did and thank God for her.

YOUR SITUATION MAY NOT CHANGE, BUT YOU CAN CHANGE.

You may be struggling with something that is literally breaking your heart. Maybe it hit you out of the blue. You just didn't see it coming at all. Here's a word from the Lord. You are being strengthened. Strength is being poured into you now. *Let us not be weary in well doing: for in due season we shall reap, if we faint not* (Galatians 6:9).

STRENGTHENED THROUGH STRUGGLE

1. **You are blessed and nobody can do anything about it**
   a. You may have to humble yourself
   b. There's a time and season for everything
   c. The perils of impatience
   d. One more time around the mountain

2. **You won't seek what you're not desperate for**
   a. King David was a man after God's own heart—desperate for God
   b. Don't spend a lifetime trying to be what you weren't created to be
   c. You cannot pray your struggles away
   d. Trouble is no respecter of persons
   e. It takes more faith to walk through than to be delivered from a struggle
   f. The patterns of our lives

3. **You can't move forward when you're paralyzed**
   a. You can have the desire to serve God and still be filled with pain
   b. Are you stuck in a cycle of pain?
   c. Forget the past and press forward
   d. What "keeping the faith" really means

4. **Cry out to God**
   a. You'll have to fight hard to make it
   b. Be transparent
   c. Three things you can't touch in God's Word
   d. There is safety and shelter from the enemy—you can make it

HOMEWORK ASSIGNMENT

Husbands and wives

1. Spend thirty minutes together this week identifying ways that God has blessed your marriage.

2. Define ways in which each of you has been strengthened through struggle.

3. Make a pact: agree to put the past behind and press forward with new resolve to be especially supportive of your spouse the next time your marriage is faced with a challenge. Put the agreement in writing, sign it, and tuck it away in a safe place. Set aside a specific time each month to refer to the agreement and discuss the improvements in your relationship since you made the agreement.

Lord, I am desperate for more of You. Your Word promises to perfect that which concerns me. I lift up my struggles to You, Father, and thank You for Your divine intervention in my marriage and family. Thank You for the strength and faith it takes to walk through family challenges. I praise You for giving Your angels charge over my home to defend and preserve my family in all our ways. I trust in You as my refuge and fortress. I put past mistakes behind me and forge ahead with peace and joy toward the good life that You have prepared for me. I praise You that my marriage is growing stronger every day because I have chosen to follow You. I call my family blessed of the Lord and give You all praise, glory, and honor. In Jesus' mighty name, I pray. Amen.

eight

CONFLICT RESOLUTION: BE ANGRY AND SIN NOT

Paula: In our experience as pastors, counseling about-to-be married couples as well as those who have many years of marriage under their belts, we have found that the cement in marriage—the glue that holds couples together—is their ability to properly resolve conflict. In fact, the first question Randy asks in a counseling session is, "Have you had a fight yet?"

Why does he ask that question first? Because life throws us a variety of conflicts and challenges, and how we resolve those problems will determine whether or not we remain together.

Surprisingly, in observing a couple that has what we call a temperament of ten (meaning the volume in their household is loud), you might think they're the ones who have all the problems. Actually, those marriages stay together just as long as the silent ones as long as both people resolve conflict with equal volume. You get into trouble when one has a volume of one and the other has a volume of ten. Obviously, the louder partner may overwhelm the one whose volume is only one, and the result is often intimidation, fear, and even abuse.

Randy: Many, many people are angry these days. They're angry with their spouse, their children, their boss, other drivers on their way to work (now described as "road rage"), their in-laws, neighbors, and co-workers. Webster defines *anger* as "a strong passion or emotion, excited by injury; rage; to incite to wrath or displease."

We're going to start right here with scriptures that specifically address the subject of anger and go from there. Ephesians 4:26,27 AMP says, *When angry, do not sin; do not ever let your wrath (your exasperation, your fury or indignation) last until the sun goes down. Leave no [such] room or foothold for the devil [give no opportunity to him].* Notice the Word of God says "*when* angry." This tells me we're all going to get angry at one time or another. Otherwise, it would say *if* we get angry. . . .

These verses also communicate that you can get angry without committing a sin. You can get angry about your bills, for example. You can become angry about poverty in your life, but you don't have to get angry about it every payday. A pattern of anger is extremely dangerous to others as well as to yourself.

The danger of mixing anger with marriage is that when people are angry they say and do things they really don't mean. Nobody knows you as well as your spouse, and he/she can hit you way below the belt. She can dig up things during an argument that you forgot years ago. Then you retaliate and say something hurtful and painful to her. And the fight is on. You and I have to learn how to harness anger, and I'm going to show you how to do that.

When anger is directed in the right way, you can actually harness its explosive energy to accomplish a great deal. But you must begin by learning to control your temper. Many people—and I believe men particularly—have been taught some wrong behavior patterns by their own fathers. Often men (more than women, I think) allow hurts to build and fester. We allow resentments to gain a hold over us, and we don't easily forgive and forget. And men are better at hiding their emotions than women. We act as though nothing can hurt us—we're big, tough, and macho. We don't like to admit we have feelings that *can* be hurt.

The longer we allow an offense to fester, the more our anger builds and the more violent it's going to become. There is a spiritual solution to this. You go to the person who offended you and get it resolved. Deal with the issue within a twenty-four-hour period—do not wait—it is the formula to obtaining victory over anger.

Some of the things you're still angry about happened so long ago that you can't even remember what started it. Nobody is really sure now what started the legendary feud between the Hatfields and McCoys, but it consumed entire generations of people who weren't even involved in the original dispute. Foolish and ridiculous, isn't it? But what's the difference between them and you, if you haven't turned loose of your anger and never dealt with the issues that caused it?

Don't take your grievance to everybody else either. Go straight to the person who hurt or offended you, and deal with the issue eyeball to eyeball. Don't hide it under a rug. Bring it to light. The devil loves to keep things hidden. Refuse to play his game.

Unresolved anger will affect you spiritually and physically. There are people who are sick today because they have not dealt with issues of anger. Why carry that destructive spirit of anger around? Let's get victory over it once and for all.

YOU CAN'T *MAKE* ANYBODY MAD

Anger is the only emotion the Bible says you had better take care of swiftly. Have you ever said to your spouse (or anyone else), "You *make* me so mad?" You can't make anybody mad. You *choose* to be mad. My wife taught me this years ago.

UNRESOLVED ANGER WILL AFFECT YOU SPIRITUALLY AND PHYSICALLY.

When we first started our church, our building was egged. Some people didn't want us around, so they tried to discourage us by throwing eggs at our building. You've never seen such a mess. Paula said, "If you want to get even with them, just be successful. Don't let them know you're angry. Don't give in to that spirit."

If you were a witness as a child to angry arguments that resulted in your father hitting your mother, it doesn't mean you have to behave in the same way with your wife. Just because you regularly heard your father swearing at your mother doesn't mean that this is a proper way to communicate your opinion or disapproval.

I've said it before, and I'll say it again—the Bible deals with everything we'll ever need to know about anything. The apostle Paul's letter to the church at Ephesus offers a practical explanation of how to treat your spouse:

Let no foul or polluting language, nor evil word nor unwholesome or worthless talk [ever] come out of your mouth, but only such [speech] as is good and beneficial to the spiritual progress of others, as is fitting to the need and the occasion, that it may be a blessing and give grace (God's favor) to those who hear it, Paul says to the Ephesians in chapter 4 and verse 29 AMP.

Verses 30-32 go on to say, *And do not grieve the Holy Spirit of God [do not offend or vex or sadden Him], by Whom you were sealed (marked, branded as God's own, secured) for the day of redemption (of final deliverance through Christ from evil and the consequences of sin). Let all bitterness and indignation and wrath (passion, rage, bad temper) and resentment (anger, animosity) and quarreling (brawling, clamor, contention) and slander (evil-speaking, abusive or blasphemous language) be banished from you, with all malice (spite, ill will, or baseness of any kind). And become useful and helpful and kind to one another, tenderhearted (compassionate, understanding, loving-hearted), forgiving one another [readily and freely], as God in Christ forgave you.*

In other words, you can afford to show your spouse and children grace because God has showered His grace on you. I don't know about you, but I need all the grace I can get. I am willing to be very generous with grace and mercy toward Paula, our kids, the staff at the church, and everyone with whom I come in contact. Why? Because God is the God of a second chance. I never want to be the kind of person who refuses to be generous in giving grace and mercy when I've been on the receiving end of so much grace and mercy myself.

BE GENEROUS IN GIVING GRACE AND MERCY.

Hypocrisy makes me angry. If you come into my office for counseling and act like you're the only one at your house who knows how to do anything and your wife or husband is always wrong, I get just a little suspicious. When people come in and tell me they've done the best they can to teach and train their spouse to be like them (because they're always right, you know), I start thinking, *Whoa, there. Something's definitely out of line here. If you had the answers to every problem, God would be out of a job!*

Don't come to my office and tell me you're living one way, then walk out and live a different life in front of your wife (husband) and children. Folks like that are like a chameleon. They change colors for whomever they're around. That's hypocrisy, and it makes me angry.

ALL HOUSEHOLDS ARE BILINGUAL

We've already discussed the differences between men and women, but I address this again relative to the subject of anger because men and women speak two entirely different languages. Paula says all households are bilingual: manspeak and womanspeak. They may not realize it, but husbands and wives (a.k.a. men and women) each have a language all their own. I don't know why God did that, but He did.

Paula and I have been married a long time now, and to this very day she still asks me what I did all day the minute I walk in the door, even though she knows it irritates me. I like to unwind a little when I get home. I want to eat, and then I want to rest. I want to leave my work at the office. But Paula doesn't want that. She wants to talk about the day's events in detail. And she finds out the details of what I've done one way or another.

One Valentine's Day a few years ago, I wanted to do something nice for Paula, so I gave my associate pastor my credit card and asked him to take care of seeing to it that Paula got some roses. The bottom line—to my way of thinking—was that she got the roses. I thought she would be all lovey-dovey that afternoon when I got home because she loves to get flowers.

I was feeling good inside because I had remembered Valentine's Day and actually arranged for something I was sure she would like. I walked in the door thinking I'd done well and we were going to have a nice evening together. I couldn't have been more wrong!

When I walked in, Paula said, "You didn't stop what you were doing today and go get those roses, did you? It doesn't mean anything to me unless you went and got the roses yourself." I was in trouble over something I thought was going to turn out great! And women never forget. Have you noticed this? In an argument, they have this way of reaching back twenty years and retrieving some priceless piece of memorabilia that you can't even remember, such as all the Valentine's Days (and other holidays) you've forgotten.

Anyway, on this occasion, Paula was angry, and I was angry. Valentine's Day that year didn't turn out to be very romantic at all.

THE ANGER TEST

Let's take a pop quiz. You only have to answer "yes" or "no." If you're a husband, I'm telling you right now, you have to answer these questions for yourself—you don't want your wife doing this for you.

1. I am impatient more frequently than I would like.   Yes   No

2. I nurture critical thoughts quite easily.   Yes   No

3. When I am displeased with someone, I may shut
   down any communications or withdraw.   Yes   No

4. I feel inwardly annoyed when family and friends
   do not comprehend my needs.   Yes   No

5. Tension mounts within me as I tackle a demanding
   task.   Yes   No

6. I feel frustrated when I see someone else having fewer
   struggles than I have.   Yes   No

7. When facing an important event, I may obsessively
   ponder how I must manage it.   Yes   No

8. Sometimes I walk in another direction to avoid seeing someone I don't like. Yes No

9. When discussing a controversial topic, my tone of voice is likely to become persuasive. Yes No

10. I can accept a person who admits his or her mistakes, but I have a hard time accepting someone who refuses to admit his or her weaknesses. Yes No

11. When I talk about my irritations, I don't really want to hear an opposite point of view. Yes No

12. I do not easily forget when someone does me wrong. Yes No

13. When someone confronts me from a misinformed position, I am thinking of my rebuttal as he or she speaks. Yes No

14. Sometimes my discouragements make me want to quit. Yes No

15. I can be quite aggressive in my business pursuits or even when playing a game just for fun. Yes No

16. I struggle emotionally with the things in life that are unfair. Yes No

17. Although I know I may not be right, I sometimes blame others for my problems. Yes No

18. When someone openly speaks ill of me, my natural response is to think of how I can defend myself. Yes No

19. Sometimes I speak slanderously about a person, not really caring how it might harm his or her reputation.   Yes   No

20. I may act kindly on the outside while feeling frustrated on the inside.   Yes   No

21. I have a habit of expressing sarcasm hidden in humor.   Yes   No

22. When someone is clearly annoyed with me, I too easily jump into the conflict.   Yes   No

23. At times I struggle with moods of depression and discouragement.   Yes   No

24. I've been known to take an "I don't care" attitude toward the needs of others.   Yes   No

25. When I am in an authority role, I may speak too sternly or be insensitive.   Yes   No

Count all of your affirmative (Yes) answers. If you have checked "Yes" ten times or more, your anger is probably more constant than you are comfortable admitting. If you have answered "Yes" to more than fifteen statements, it indicates that you are vulnerable to extreme ill-effects of anger, rage, guilt, bitterness, and resentment. If you checked all of the statements with a "Yes," come to my church in Tampa, Florida, and let me lay hands on you.

No one else needs to see the results of this quiz. You never have to share your answers with anyone. That's between you and God. But use the quiz to identify some things about yourself that you may have previously overlooked. This information can be helpful to you if you allow it to be.

THE FIVE PHASES OF ANGER: IRRITATION, INDIGNATION, WRATH, FURY, AND RAGE

Psychologists have noted that there are five types of anger. Anger begins as *irritation*, which is defined as "a feeling of minor discomfort." It's okay to be irritated—there isn't anything wrong with it. In fact, some types of irritation are good because they can stimulate change for the better.

Have you and your mate ever been irritated about something—maybe with each other or your children while on your way to church? Different things irritate different people. I believe one of the greatest challenges in relationships stems from wanting our own way and becoming irritated when everybody doesn't agree with us. But as we allow God's love to flow through us we can love His way.

First Corinthians 13:4,5 AMP says, *Love endures long and is patient and kind; love never is envious nor boils over with jealousy, is not boastful or vainglorious, does not display itself haughtily. It is not conceited (arrogant and inflated with pride); it is not rude (unmannerly) and does not act unbecomingly. Love (God's love in us) does not insist on its own rights or its own way, for it is not self-seeking; it is not touchy or fretful or resentful; it takes no account of the evil done to it [it pays no attention to a suffered wrong].*

Indignation is another type of anger described by psychologists. It is interpreted as "frustration over something that is unfair or unreasonable." If someone slices your tires, for example, you are quite likely to become both irritated and indignant. I can assure you that I would be. You can become indignant when your refrigerator conks out the day after the warranty expires . . . or when a tire blows out on your way home from having your car serviced. You were assured that everything on the car checked out—they said you were good for another 3,000 miles before you'd have to come in again! It's unfair! It's not right! You're absolutely correct, but these things happen, and we have to learn to adjust.

Next—and here's where I really want to dwell—is wrath. *Wrath* is a phase of anger defined as "a strong desire to avenge or punish." Now we're getting into dangerous territory. Both irritation and indignation can be okay—they have the ability to bring about change for good—but wrath is something else entirely. It must be said, too, that both irritation and indignation can lead to wrath, but that's when they cross the line of acceptability. Hear what I am saying.

I realize that nobody can hurt you like your spouse can hurt you. He/she can say things that can bring wrath into the situation. And you begin to respond by saying and doing things you'll regret. When you take matters into your own hands and begin to plot revenge against your spouse, the likelihood that you'll lose control and irreparably endanger your relationship comes into play.

Wrath leads to fury. *Fury* is "a state that suggests violence and a temporary loss of control." We know that Jesus said you can be angry if you don't get into sin, but when anger leads to wrath and fury, sin won't be far behind. I'm convinced that when anger moves to the fury phase, that's when murders take place. People just lose control, and they don't think about what they've done until later.

Some people discipline their children in wrath and fury. Parents get angry, and many times they have every right to be. When kids ignore direction and correction and either carelessly or deliberately do something wrong, even the most patient parents can become irritated about it, maybe even to the point of righteous indignation. That's reasonable. But do not attempt to correct that child when your anger has progressed to wrath, then to fury. Why? Because when you are uncontrollably angry, you can yank on that child and maybe dislocate a joint. You can smack him in the face or throw something in the heat of anger, without even realizing what you've done.

. . . WHEN ANGER LEADS TO WRATH AND FURY, SIN WON'T BE FAR BEHIND.

Ephesians 6:4 AMP encourages fathers to avoid irritating and provoking children to anger . . . *[do not exasperate them to resentment], but rear them [tenderly] in the training and discipline and the counsel and admonition of the Lord.*

The best thing to do is wait until your anger has dissipated somewhat and you've regained control of yourself. I believe in spanking, as I've said before. I have spanked Bradley, but not when I was angry. I don't punish that child until I have my temper under control. I tell him how much I love him and that the reason I'm spanking him is because I love him.

When I'm finished, I hug him and reiterate why he is being disciplined. I'd much rather discipline him this way now than to see him in prison later, and regret that I never disciplined him properly. On the other hand, acting out of rage will foster rebellion in a child. If he sees you out of control, he'll pick up on your bad behavior and copy it in his adult life. Children may come to believe that conflict resolution starts at the end of a fist or a foul tongue, cursing and humiliating family members via the mouth.

I have scripture to back me up. Proverbs 16:32 AMP says, *He who is slow to anger is better than the mighty, he who rules his [own] spirit than he who takes a city.*

Look with me at Proverbs 19:11 AMP, *Good sense makes a man restrain his anger, and it is his glory to overlook a transgression or an offense.* In other words, put anger or wrath under control!

Watch this, Proverbs 21:19 AMP, *It is better to dwell in a desert land than with a contentious woman and with vexation.* I didn't write this. King Solomon did, and he had 900 wives, so I think he was qualified to understand the woman's psyche. Can you imagine all the PMS he had to deal with? He says, "Don't get upset, guys. Just head out to the desert for a while. This too shall pass."

Proverbs 29:22 AMP says, *A man of wrath stirs up strife, and a man given to anger commits and causes much transgression.* He's a stirrer. He has unsettled issues in his own life and takes his frustration out on others.

Ecclesiastes 7:9 AMP is another good one, *Do not be quick in spirit to be angry or vexed, for anger and vexation lodge in the bosom of fools.*

I haven't always controlled my anger well. When Paula and I first moved from Washington, D.C. to Tampa, we didn't have any money at all. We were so poor that the poor people called us poor. We spelled poor with three o's instead of two. One time when Bradley hurt his arm, we couldn't take him to Tampa General Hospital for x-rays, so we took him to the airport to go through their x-ray machine to determine whether or not his arm was broken! Now, that's bad! I was angry because I couldn't provide for our son's needs.

Financial pressure makes you do funny stuff. When you don't have the money to take care of life's necessities, you can get so angry that you might cross over into wrath and fury and do something really stupid.

Around that time someone gave us twenty dollars. I wanted to go to Jimbo's Pit Barbecue, and Paula wanted to go to Taco Bell. It had been a long time since we'd had money to go anywhere.

Paula: We were so poor, and as soon as I heard about the twenty-dollar gift, I started doing some strategic planning. We had not been out on a "date" for more than a year because we had no money. If we ever got our hands on any cash, we had bills to pay. You know the drill. It was all we could do to have food on our table at that time.

So I thought this was wonderful—we could go out on a date. As a woman, this meant a great deal to me. I thought, *We can go to Taco Bell and get cheap, but good, burritos and then go to a movie, all for twenty dollars. Matinees are cheaper than going to the show in the evening, and we can share one box of popcorn . . . we can do it all!*

Although I knew Randy hated Taco Bell, I thought their prices fit nicely into the budget for our dream date. The restaurant where he wanted to go would take the whole twenty dollars just to eat, so I insisted on Taco Bell so that we could also go to the show. Finally Randy reluctantly agreed to go to Taco Bell.

When we got to the restaurant, he looked at the price of burritos and ordered twenty! He was determined to spend the entire twenty dollars because he was so mad that I'd gotten my way. I was so mad because he'd spent all our money on burritos that I made him eat every single one of them!

Randy: She did! She made me eat all twenty of those burritos. Now, why did I bring all of this up? Because if the truth were known, you have similar stories to tell. You've done stupid things in a fit of anger. You've locked each other out of the house, put bleach in a load of laundry, etc. We cross over into fury, and we don't even remember how it happened.

Now Paula and I never argue. We just have disagreements that can be heard forty miles away, but we never argue. If you get into an argument with your spouse, you don't have to put your fist through the wall and curse. You can get angry, but you can deal with it, resolve the conflict, and move on. That scripture in Ephesians 4: 26 AMP about getting angry but not sinning goes on to include this instruction, . . . *do not ever let your wrath . . . last until the sun goes down.*

When you're mad at your husband or wife, it is very difficult to resolve that conflict before dark. You get in bed on your side, he/she gets in bed on the other side, you put the covers between you and say, "Don't touch me." This is definitely not conducive to a good night's sleep. If you don't resolve that thing before bedtime, it lingers on and on. You wake up with it the next day, and the next day, and the next. You need to get the problem resolved before it grows into something bigger than both of you.

A story recently made headlines around the state of Florida. The wife of a minister pastoring a successful church near St. Petersburg stabbed him to death, and she was arrested for murder. If you could talk with her today, she would probably tell you that she does not remember what happened. In the heat of the moment, something was said, and she took a big butcher knife, struck him in the leg, severed a main artery, and he bled to death in his bed.

Two years before, he had admitted to having committed adultery. That thing festered in her, and she had never dealt with her anger toward him for this ungodly indiscretion. If only she could have controlled the wrath that led to her fury, she wouldn't be where she is today.

... GET THE PROBLEM RESOLVED BEFORE IT GROWS INTO SOMETHING BIGGER THAN BOTH OF YOU.

The most dangerous phase of anger is the fifth and final one on our list. It is rage. *Rage* is a condition that can cause people to become violent to the point that they are scarcely aware of what they are doing. They destroy property and people. Webster says *rage* is "a short period of great anger; raving fury; great force or violence, as of the wind; to be violent and out of control [a raging storm; a fire raging through the forest]; to show extreme anger."

This pastor's wife is in jail because of a spirit of wrath and rage. Who gets the glory? Satan. The pastor is dead, his wife is in jail, the church is split up, and the blessings of the Lord are long gone.

Who would have thought we would have to provide counseling today for a condition known as *road rage?* A driver cuts someone off on the interstate, and that person retaliates by pulling out a gun and killing the supposed offender! This is a ridiculous but serious issue, and we have to deal with it as a body of believers.

Have you ever said or done anything in anger that you regretted? I'm sure you have. Almost everyone has some regrets about how we've treated some person. Hopefully, it has not resulted in danger to another individual.

You are a product of what you hang around. The reason some folks act as they do relates to the people they associate with. If you hang around liars, guess what's going to happen? There are certain things that I cannot do because it would cause me to sin. I haven't always been a Christian. There are certain songs that remind me of things, places, and people that I don't want any dealings with. I've gained victory over that a long time ago, and I'm not going back there.

You have no business getting with your friends if it causes you to stumble. I was in the airport just the other day. I travel a lot, and sometimes I feel as though I live at the airport. One day I saw a preacher there who I've known for years. He didn't realize that anybody was around who knew him. He was looking through the pornography rack!

If you have a problem with pornography, stay away from it. If you have a problem with drinking, don't get with your old drinking buddies. It's going to pull you back down. If you get around someone who's angry all the time, that spirit is going to get over on you. You need to be around Holy

Ghost-filled people. Stick with people who are going to lift you up and build you up, and not tear you down.

As pastors, we've seen women in our church who have been beaten half to death by their husbands because of wrath, fury, and rage. There's something wrong with that. You may disagree with me, and that's perfectly all right, but I advise these women to leave husbands like that. God does not expect anyone to live in a relationship where she is being abused in this way.

I have no problem telling the men in my church that they have no right to hit their wives. I know it's easy to get angry. Your wife can push all the wrong buttons, and if you allow yourself to get enraged, before you know what's happened you've broken her nose, her ribs, and blackened her eye. You have to get victory over that temper. Just stop, take a deep breath, step away from the situation for a moment, and collect your thoughts. Use your head to rationalize what's going on. Look at the situation from your spouse's perspective and calm down. God will help you do that.

Paula: I've learned what not to say to Randy White to incite an angry reaction. He's learned not to push the button on my very last nerve. The fruit of the Spirit is self-control, and we operate in it.

Randy: You may need to repent to your wife (husband). Do it right now. Don't put it off. Get on top of that anger. Learn how to resolve conflict in your marriage. Your marriage and family are worth it.

The world will tell you that conflict resolution can be achieved by something called primal therapy. Therapists try to take you back to your childhood where someone abused you. When you get to that place in your mind, you are to get into the fetal position and do something called a primal scream.

People pay as much as $150 an hour to reach the place where they can experience this primal scream. Well, I'm not very impressed with this psychological nonsense. Let me tell you, all you're going to get out of a primal scream is a sore throat! It won't bring you victory because screaming won't eradicate the pain. Only the blood of Jesus can do that for you.

Don't pass a spirit of anger down through your genes to future generations of your family. Repent to your wife, husband, parents, children, or whomever you've inflicted pain and suffering upon. Repent before God of anything you've done that is not pleasing to Him. Claim God's amazing grace. Believe that His grace is sufficient to cover you and that His mercies toward you endure forever.

Sever ungodly ties that don't bring glory to God. Refuse to listen to things that incite you to anger and potential violence. Ask God to help you to be a godly man or woman. He will help you to become Christlike in every situation. He is a good God, and He loves you!

CONFLICT RESOLUTION: BE ANGRY AND SIN NOT

1. **Randy's first question to couples in counseling: Have you had a fight yet?**
   a. How do you manage anger?
   b. Don't follow in a violent parent's footsteps
   c. Avoid bringing up past failures

2. **Paul's letter to the Ephesians addressing behavior**
   a. Avoid saying and doing things you'll regret later
   b. Be generous with grace and mercy—God has been merciful to you
   c. All households are bilingual: manspeak and womanspeak

3. **The anger test**
   a. 25 Important Questions: Just a "Yes" or a "No" will do
   b. Identify your strengths and weaknesses, and ask God to help you

4. **The five phases of anger**
   a. Irritation
   b. Indignation
   c. Wrath
   d. Fury
   e. Rage

HOMEWORK ASSIGNMENT

Husbands and Wives

1. How do you and your spouse reach solutions to your differences? Do you fight fair? Think about it individually, and then talk about it together.

2. Set aside time to discuss ways each of you could communicate your issues in a more positive way than you have in the past.

Father, Your Word declares that when we come to You, we become a new creation. According to Romans 12:1, I present myself as a living sacrifice, holy and acceptable unto You. Crucify those things in my flesh that trigger anger, malice, and wrath. Let the fruit of Your Spirit of self-control be manifested in me. Help me to yield myself to You, O Lord. Mold me into the image of Christ, knowing that as I come to You, You will enable me to control those things that would try to control me. I ask these things in the matchless name of Jesus, my Lord and Savior. Amen.

nine

TWELVE SPIES, PERCEPTION, AND THE VIRTUOUS WOMAN

Paula: I have been given wonderful opportunities to teach and preach—often to women—and frequently I deal with issues that especially concern women. One crucial issue I teach about is perception. The biblical foundation I build on is Numbers 13, which is a study on Israel's disobedience.

In Numbers 13, God has led the nation of Israel to the border of Canaan, where the people were *commanded* to enter the land and take it from its inhabitants. Now, God did not just *suggest* that they take the Promised Land, and the Bible doesn't say He *instructed* them to take it. It clearly says He *commanded* them to do it—to be aggressive about it, even. "Go in there, and do what I, the Lord your God, tell you to do!"

Verses 1-25 talk about the scouts that were sent out to explore the land and bring back a report. In verses 26-33, they agree that the land is rich. They even returned with samples of the abundant produce! But ten of the scouts fearfully described the power of the giant inhabitants in that region. They totally discounted the power of God—the one who had won their freedom from Egypt by magnificent acts of power—insisting that Israel was unable to go up against those giants because they were so much stronger than they (see verse 31).

All twelve scouts served the same God, shared the same promise, and had the same opportunity to view or perceive this situation in a positive light. Ten of them, however, negatively perceived what they had seen as impossible. Only two, Joshua and Caleb, believed God would bring them through safely.

Perception is defined as "the act of understanding or becoming aware of through one of the senses, especially through seeing; to take through the mind; understand; knowledge or clear understanding achieved by seeing." Why did only two of these twelve scouts come back with a positive report?

How can a person, like me, for example, be physically and sexually abused and go on to be very successful in life, when someone else is in a mental institution as a result of identical circumstances? How can someone lose a child, go through a painful divorce, or debilitating illness and go on to become whole? Why does one individual turn her stumbling block into a stepping stone, or exchange pain for power, and someone else who experiences exactly the same terrible things end up defeated and destroyed for the rest of her life?

All of us have been given the same promises in the Word of God. We have the same opportunities to serve almighty God. So why do some make it to victory and others don't? In reference to the twelve spies, I believe that ten of them looked at the wrong thing. Like them, we tend to look at what could have been . . . or should have been. We look at the problem instead of the answer. Two of the scouts looked at the potential solution—what God could do with that situation.

It is vital that we change our focus because perception is more powerful than reality. Problems are just preparation for God's power. It's all in how you view it. I've said it before—Paul never prayed his storms away. He prayed to be strengthened in his inner man *through* the storms in order to grasp knowledge of the height, depth, and love of Christ.

So often we pray for our situation to be changed, and God is saying, "I want you to be strengthened in your inner man. Even though you are going through hell in your home, even though you don't have any money, and although your situation doesn't seem to be changing at all, real healing and wholeness is coming to you." It's not what we go through in life, but how we go through it that really counts.

The twelve spies were given the same opportunities, but ten of them said, *And there we saw the giants, the sons of Anak, which come of the giants: and we were in our own sight as grasshoppers, and so we were in their sight* (Numbers 13:33). If your perception has been affected by abuse or any other type of abnormal treatment, you unconsciously attract what you think (perceive) you deserve.

This perception plays out in your marriage, on your job, with your children, and in every relationship you've ever had and ever will have—*if* you continue to *perceive* yourself as lesser than someone else. Randy always says respect cannot be demanded—

it must be earned. It is earned because we are constantly sending out signals. I'll use myself as an example.

Although I travel a great deal without my husband, I have no trouble with men flirting with me or trying to pick me up. I don't think it's because I'm unattractive. I believe it stems from the signals I send out. I don't offer any opportunities for anyone to become familiar with me. A man is not willing to set himself up for failure. He has an ego to deal with, and it's highly unlikely that he'll put his ego on the line.

Perception is powerful. How you perceive yourself, your marriage, your family, and all other relationships is very important. Every marriage goes through different ruts. It's easy to get into a rut and just look at the dirty socks on the floor, the stack of dirty dishes in the sink, the pile of wet towels in the bathroom, and start thinking certain thoughts about your future. You're looking at the wrong thing!

You can change that perception and start thinking, "Well, my husband's not out in the bars at night. He has always been faithful to me. He works hard to support us. . . ." If you'll begin to think differently, you'll start talking differently. When you start to talk differently, your husband will begin to react to you differently. Things will change for the better! What actually happens is influenced by your perception. Understanding brings fulfillment.

IF YOU'LL BEGIN TO THINK DIFFERENTLY, YOU'LL START TALKING DIFFERENTLY.

That's why the Bible says in Hosea 4:6, *My people are destroyed for lack of knowledge.* . . . Understanding and perception—I cannot stress enough their importance.

It goes back to educating yourself. Education is power. The more knowledge you have about the person you're married to or the person you plan to marry, the more you'll understand and assimilate your differences. The more knowledge you acquire about the differences between men and women, personality differences, and what the Word of God has to say about marriage, the more successful your marriage will be. Knowledge is power—it equips you for life!

I use this as an example in counseling couples. I take a bunch of coins and throw them out on a table in front of them. I ask the man sitting at the table in front of me, "What do you see?" He says, "I see seventy-nine cents." Then I ask the woman what she sees. She says, "I see two quarters, two dimes, a nickel, and four pennies." They are looking at exactly the same coins, but they're seeing them differently! Perception is basic to the miraculous nature and structure of men and women.

This little illustration helps them understand that although they are looking at the same things, they do not necessarily perceive them identically. It helps to facilitate the marriage by bringing knowledge and understanding into the equation.

I believe every married couple—and those who are about to be married—should take a personality profile test. Randy and I think it should be in "The Rule Book," if there were such a thing. We believe it is helpful for couples to take personality profile tests prior to even the premarital counseling! Let me give you a prime example, keeping in mind that Randy and I had no knowledge of the personality profile test when we were first married.

Right after we were married, I tried to be super-wife, super-mom, and super-woman. At first we had just one child living with us. Since then we've always had two or more with us at a time, but not at first. The ministry was just getting started, and we also had a little business going on the side. I was trying to keep the house clean and make gourmet meals out of burritos because we didn't have much money.

During the day, I was Randy's church administrator, children's director, secretary, and bookkeeper. Then I rushed home, wanting to make sure Randy and Bradley had a good meal at dinnertime. I cleaned and scrubbed everything down with bleach, and one night I had everything done right on schedule, except for one small basket of laundry.

Randy walked into the house and said, "What about that laundry?" I wanted to throw it at him! Everything—and I do mean everything—else in that house was in perfect order and dinner was on the table . . . and he found the one tiny little thing that wasn't done to comment about.

A CURIOUS MIXTURE OF STRENGTHS AND WEAKNESSES IS MAN (AND WOMAN)

I've learned that Randy couldn't help it. He's choleric! That's his personality or temperament, if you will. I've learned that temperament traits are received genetically from our parents and circumstances. Tim LaHaye's wonderful book, *Spirit-Controlled Personality,* and Florence Littauer's *Your Personality Tree* literally set us free from a variety of misperceptions of each other and our marriage. We learned about the four basic temperaments—Popular Sanguine, Powerful Choleric, Perfect Melancholy, and Peaceful Phlegmatic.

Randy White is a powerful choleric. The P.C. (powerful choleric) is quick, active, practical, strong-willed, independent, and self-sufficient. He tends toward decisiveness and is very opinionated. Cholerics, like Randy, are goal-oriented leaders.

All of this information about the different personalities was a great revelation to us. I realized that Randy is sick. He's choleric! He's got a problem, you see, because he's not like me! Once I found out about this, I no longer heard, "Paula, you've failed," when Randy pointed out something I hadn't noticed. I heard, "Randy, you are an over-perfectionist."

Believe me, you'll understand so much more about why you and your mate do the things you do or react the way you react when you learn about the different personalities. It is enormously helpful in bringing clarity and understanding to the marriage relationship. When you understand that God has uniquely designed you to be who you are, while at the same time, He's designed your spouse (usually entirely differently), I believe you'll heave a huge sigh of relief. There's nothing so wrong about you (or your mate)—you're just different!

This doesn't mean that you're always right and he or she is always wrong. No! No! No! I was just kidding about Randy being sick because he's choleric. Each of the four personalities has key strengths and weaknesses. No one temperament is more desirable than another. Each makes a valuable contribution to all of our lives. When you learn about your own strengths and weaknesses as well as your spouse's—and those of your children, for that matter—your perception of things relative to the successful life of your family will quickly be clarified.

THERE'S NOTHING SO WRONG ABOUT YOU (OR YOUR MATE)— YOU'RE JUST DIFFERENT!

This knowledge has helped us so much with our children. One of our sons is very athletic. The other is very creative. They are as opposite as day and night, and it is so important that we understand their different personalities. It is especially vital in combined families. Some of our children needed more time than the others did. We learned how to deal with all of our differences from profiling our personalities.

Ours is a blended family. Randy brought three children to the marriage and I brought one. We have been so, so blessed with these children. It has been an altogether wonderful experience for all of us. Randy is about nine and a half years older than me. I was very young when we married, but I had sense enough to know that I wasn't marrying everything Randy White would become. I was marrying everything he had been. That's important to what I'm about to say.

Randy didn't have a lot of money when I met him. I knew that one day there would be a great future, and I also knew I was marrying his children. To deny your mate's past will create a lot of problems for you. You must be very realistic when you enter into a relationship that has even the potential of progressing toward marriage. Be sure to count the cost. *For which of you, intending to build a tower, sitteth not down first, and counteth the cost, whether he have sufficient to finish it?* (Luke 14:28). *And Jesus said unto him, No man, having put his hand to the plow, and looking back, is fit for the kingdom of God* (Luke 9:62). We cannot spend any time looking back and saying, "What if, what could have been, what might have been, or what should have been." Don't allow yourself to give in to the "woulda, shoulda, couldas" of life.

I knew what I was getting into. I didn't know if all the kids would live with us or not, but I knew I'd need to be a mother to four children—Randy's three and my one son. I understood each child because I had gotten to know them. I wanted to know what caused the breakup of Randy's first marriage. I believe we need to use wisdom. Why? Because "people change, but not much."

You need to know when a person goes from relationship to relationship if they're still packing around the same baggage. You need to understand why it didn't work before. Statistically, second marriages fail more often than first ones. I'm not saying they can't work because Randy and I are obviously an example of a second marriage that works. But why? You have to use wisdom and get to know your mate's children from a previous marriage so that when you say "I do" to that man, you have said "Yes" to his children.

Discuss the responsibilities your blended family will produce. Deal with the issue of child support, for example. Child support often places

> "PEOPLE CHANGE, BUT NOT MUCH."

financial hardship on second marriages—decide how that will affect you. Seek wise counsel. Be realistic and responsible. Know what you are getting yourself into. Don't be blindly led by love. One week after that honeymoon is over you're going to be paying bills. It will be reality time.

Randy and I have a different relationship with each of our four children. Just a while back, my 15-year-old son Brad, who has been raised by Randy since he was one year old, was experiencing some challenges at school, and he got a little more smart-mouthed with me than he would have with his father. Randy sat him down and said, "Now, son, she is my wife before she's your mother. No one will speak to my wife like that."

From the very beginning of our relationship, Randy established with all of our children that I am his wife first. This is especially important with blended families because there is a great potential for everyone to try and stake out a measure of control over things. Once it was established that I am Randy's wife first and their mother second, it communicated to our kids that Brad needn't spend time running to me for help with Randy, and Randy's children didn't need to bother running to him for help with me.

Woman of God . . .
A Masterpiece Called Virtuous

Proverbs 31:10-31 describes a woman of virtue. *Virtue* means "goodness; right action and thinking; morality; chastity; purity; good qualities; merit." The Hebrew word for virtue, *chayil,* means "strong in all mental and moral qualities." In other words, she's strong emotionally, spiritually, and physically—a real "got it together" woman whose strength is a result of her great faith, her family, and her finances!

I compared this woman to another famous woman of the Bible, the Luke 8:43 woman—the woman with the issue of blood. Note the differences. The Luke 8:43 woman was weak in her faith, her family, and her finances. The reason she was weak in her faith was because she'd been raised with a heathen background. She'd gone through a situation for a long time in her family. She'd been separated from everyone because of her infirmity—perhaps even her family had grown weary of caring for her . . . having to carry in meals and help her to bed. Her finances were depleted because of her infirmity—she'd spent all of her money on physicians and medicine.

The faith, family, and finances that strengthened the Proverbs 31 woman brought the Luke 8:43 woman to such a point of desperation that she had to do something on her own. She had heard about Jesus and what happened whenever He came around, and in her desperation, she decided—*If only I can touch Him, I'll be healed.* Her faith made the leap all the way from her house to where Jesus was, so that by the time she arrived, all she had to do was touch Him and she was made whole.

It has been my heart's desire to be a woman of God. I began to look through the Word to find examples, mentors, and leaders to define my life and habits. In my search, the Proverbs 31 woman of virtue stands out as *the* woman. Who is she? What makes her who she is? How do I *become* her? My research revealed the following facts that I hope will be as helpful to you as they have been to me.

The only other person specifically identified as a virtuous woman in the Bible is Ruth. Chapter 3, verse 11 says, *And now, my daughter, fear not; I will do to thee all that thou requirest: for all the city of my people doth know that thou art a virtuous woman.*

CHARACTERISTICS OF A VIRTUOUS WOMAN FROM PROVERBS 31

1. **Morally Strong** She has strong convictions; ethics. She is upright and not double-minded. She is able to discern between good and evil (v.12).

2. **Invaluable** Her price is far above rubies. This is not the description of every woman but of a "few" women. Some things

cannot be bought. A good woman is hard to find—rare, unlike the masses (v.10).

3. **Trustworthy** Her husband has absolute confidence in her faithfulness. If she is told something in confidence, she keeps it. She is definitely not a busybody or one who gossips. She is neither deceitful nor manipulative (v.11).

4. **Inherently good and true** She does good to her husband and not evil all the days of her life. Since her personal characteristics are not based on the way he treats her or her circumstances, she does good at all times. She does not have a "Plan B" in case things are not going the way she thinks they should. Her agenda, clear and concise, is to do good! (v.12).

5. **Ingenious/proficient** She is creative. She finds one more way to prepare the leftover chicken. She loves to work. She thinks productivity/achiever. She works willfully and cheerfully with her hands. She knows there is more to life than getting out of bed and waiting for her husband to come home at 5:30 (v.13).

6. **Thrifty/laborious** She looks for the best deals, utilizing sales, coupons, bargains, and is not frivolous (v.14).

7. **Dutiful/considerate** She is loving and takes care of her own household first. She then considers the needs of others and takes care of them. She is flexible. She does not get all bent out of shape when her husband brings dinner guests home at the last minute (v.15).

8. **Versatile/judicious** She is not afraid to venture into a new business to provide for her growing family. She is informed on current events and situations. She will do what she has never done to get what she has never had (v.16).

9. **Tireless/healthy** She keeps herself and her family in perfect health with proper food and clothing. She takes care of herself with proper rest, nutrition, and exercise (v.17).

10. **Joyful/efficient** She is honest and upright in all of her business dealings. She has a PMA (positive mental attitude). The joy of the Lord is her strength (v.17).

11. **Watchful/cautious** She does not make hasty decisions (v.18).

12. **Thrifty/skillful** She has a trade. She knows how to do something! Find out where your gifts and talents are and develop them. Build on the abilities God gave you. Flow in your purpose and you will fulfill your destiny. Don't major on your minors (v.19).

13. **Charitable/benevolent** She respects and loves both God and the poor and is as good as she is capable of being to all who are in need. She is a giver (v.20).

> FLOW IN YOUR PURPOSE AND YOU WILL FULFILL YOUR DESTINY.

14. **Generous/merciful** She has a heart to take care of the poor and needy. Jesus said, . . . *Verily I say unto you, Inasmuch as ye have done it unto one of the least of these my brethren, ye have done it unto me* (Matthew 25:40) [v.20].

15. **Fearless/provident** She is not afraid of upcoming "seasons" in her life. She is always prepared. She has the "goods" inside to face whatever life may bring her. Everyone is going to go through different tests and trials, but how do you act when you are going through them? (v.21).

16. **Clever at decorating and furnishing** She makes her house a home. You would feel welcome and warm in her home. She does not have just a slab of wood and a picture on the wall, but she is creative on whatever her budget allows. Her family is proud to bring guests over (v.22).

17. **Refined in taste** This refers to her clothing. She knows her apparel is a reflection of her husband as well as a statement about how she feels about herself. She chooses her clothing carefully. In other words, she does not wear stripes with checks. In the Italian and Jewish cultures, the way a woman dressed was a reflection on the success of her husband. The Bible records that you are the glory of your husband. How are you portraying your husband? (v.22).

18. **Respected/popular** Refers to her husband being known and respected in public, not only because of his position but also because of being the husband of a woman held in high esteem. How would you like it if your husband were "most popular" because he is married to a virtuous woman? (v.23).

19. **Industrious/prosperous** She is creative with the gifts and talents that God has given to her. Unlike the unfaithful servant who took his talent and buried it in the ground, the Proverbs 31 woman knows how to take what is in her hand and multiply it— not for selfish gain but to bless her family and her church. Proverbs 10:4 says, *He becometh poor that dealeth with a slack hand: but the hand of the diligent maketh rich.* She is not lazy. She will roll up her sleeves and do whatever it takes to get the job done. She is a hard worker and productive (v.24).

20. **Dependable/honest** She is reliable. She does not have hidden motives. When she gives her word, you know you can count on her. She does not speak "little white lies." If she says she will be there or she will do something, she will. She does not start a project and walk away from it, leaving it unfinished. If she gives her word to greet at church or teach Sunday School, she will stay true to her word (v.25).

21. **Confident/hopeful** Her confidence and self-esteem are not centered on her talents and abilities but on the God who

gives them to her. Second Timothy 1:12 says, . . . *for I know whom I have believed, and am persuaded that he is able to keep that which I have committed unto him against that day.* In times of trial she finds inner strength, hope, and peace because all that she has, she commits to the Lord. Even in the midst of trials, she knows she will rejoice in times to come (v.25).

22. **Wise/discreet** *She opens her mouth in skillful and godly Wisdom, and on her tongue is the law of kindness [giving counsel and instruction].* The virtuous woman is an example of a meek and quiet spirit. Meek, however, does not imply that people walk all over her and that she is afraid to speak truth. The definition of *meek* is simply "controlled strength." She considers her words and does not speak rashly. Proverbs 15:1 says, *A soft answer turneth away wrath: but grievous words stir up anger.* She understands that her mouth is an instrument of praise and that she is accountable for every idle word. She lives by the rule that if her words do not comfort, edify, or exhort, she does not speak them (v.26 AMP).

23. **Kind/understanding** She has a sweet disposition. She knows how to encourage others in their time of need. She is the type of woman you would seek for counsel, because your heart safely trusts her and you know that she will neither judge you nor speak against you (v.26).

24. **Prudent/practical** Her house and her children are her priority. She manages her household with economy and discretion. Her children are well-behaved and keep good company. She teaches practical skills that lead to a successful life by emphasizing order in the home. She ministers to her children—spirit, soul, and body (v.27).

25. **Energetic/ever-active** She is not lazy. She carefully plans her day and seeks the Lord for direction. She cannot afford to sleep until noon, watch soap operas, and spend hours gossiping

on the phone. She rises early and understands that "this is the day that the Lord has made. . . ." It takes energy to produce energy. She exercises because of her busy schedule, realizing that exercise produces more energy and makes you feel great about yourself. It gets oxygen to your brain! (v.27).

26. **An ideal wife and mother** Her husband is first in her life, and he knows it. She thinks ahead of ways she can be a helpmeet to him. She quickly lays down her agenda to pick up his. She brings security to her children by loving her husband. Her children do not lack because of material or emotional needs. She sees that a good education comes next to a relationship with God (v.28).

27. **Honored by her family** Her family esteems her highly and appreciates her hard work and sacrifices to make their house a home. They don't wait until Mother's Day to demonstrate their appreciation. They continuously praise her. Appreciation and praise are the inevitable result of a virtuous woman. Her family has to "ooooh" and "ahhhhhh" about her because she is a model of someone who is consistent, strong, wise, comforting, and virtuous (vv.27,28).

28. **Excels in virtue** She has the mind of Christ, therefore, she imparts godly traits into her children. She leads by example, teaching them the importance of integrity, commitment, faithfulness, meekness, and holiness (v.29).

29. **Godfearing/humble** God's Word says, *Humble yourselves therefore under the mighty hand of God, that he may exalt you in due time* (1 Peter 5:6). The virtuous woman clothes herself with humility. She does not think of herself higher than she ought to. She is humble before God. Humility is not an outward adorning (what you wear, etc.) but rather an attitude of the heart (v.30).

30. **Deserving/successful** The secret of her success is found in the fact that in everything, she puts God first. As a result of doing this, He will crown her efforts with success (v.30).

31. **Honored by the public** Because of what she does and what she stands for, the community and neighborhood around her take note and praise her. Not only does she better herself and her family, but also she is an asset to the community in which she lives (v.31).

I have attempted to look to the Proverbs 31 woman as a role model. I have carefully examined her life and used it to reflect into my own life. Proverbs 27:17 declares, *Iron sharpeneth iron; so a man sharpeneth the countenance of his friend.* The virtuous woman described in Proverbs 31 has been my blade, so to speak, to sharpen my life as a woman.

I challenge you to believe God today to begin to cut out every area of your life that would separate you from becoming all that He has purposed you to be. You can no longer use the excuse that you are a lousy wife and mother because your mother was a lousy wife and mother. That may have been the case, but God has given you a new example. You can break the curse and become all that God intends for you to be!

How do you get there? Romans 12:2 AMP shows us the way. It says, *Do not be conformed to this world (this age), [fashioned after and adapted to its external, superficial customs], but be transformed (changed) by the [entire] renewal of your mind [by its new ideals and its new attitude], so that you may prove [for yourselves] what is the good and acceptable and perfect will of God, even the thing which is good and acceptable and perfect [in His sight for you].*

I define the word *conformed* as "to follow to a better example." Webster's says *conformed* means "to act or be in compliance;

to behave in accordance with prevailing modes or customs; to bring into agreement or correspondence." Watch who you hang out with.

Transformed means "to change in nature, function, the condition of; convert; to alter markedly by appearance or form." I call the transformation of a person a metamorphosis. A caterpillar transformed into a butterfly is a metamorphosis. God will transform you into a virtuous woman as you renew your mind with His Word!

TWELVE SPIES, PERCEPTION, AND THE VIRTUOUS WOMAN

1. **Numbers 13 and the issue of perception**
   a. All twelve scouts served the same God, shared the same promise, and had the same opportunity to perceive their situation in a positive light
   b. Only two believed God would bring them through
   c. Perception defined
   d. Perception is more powerful than reality

2. **A curious mixture of strengths and weaknesses is man (and woman)**
   a. Revelation of the four personality traits: Choleric, Sanguine, Melancholy, and Phlegmatic
   b. Blended families
   c. Assessing the baggage
   d. Women are wives first and mothers second

3. **Woman of God . . . a masterpiece called virtuous**
   a. Virtue defined in the Proverbs 31 woman
   b. A comparison of the Proverbs 31 woman and the Luke 8:43 woman
   c. Thirty-one definitive characteristics of a virtuous woman
   d. You can be transformed!

Homework Assignment

1. Don't put this off. Go to your local library or Christian bookstore and obtain a copy of Florence Littauer's *Your Personality Tree* and Tim LaHaye's *Spirit-Controlled Temperament*. Assess your own personality, your mate's traits, and those of your children. It will help you perceive each other better!

2. Use Proverbs 31 as a daily devotion for one month. Don't just read it—meditate on the verse of the day. Allow the definitive characteristics of the Proverbs 31 woman to transform you into the virtuous beauty you've always dreamed of being! Proverbs 31 is written all over you, honey!

Father, in Jesus' name, I ask You to clarify my perception of my spouse, myself, and our children. I believe that perception is, indeed, more powerful than reality, and I confess to You, Lord, that I have not always seen things as clearly as I could and should have. Thank You for delivering me from myself! Thank You for depositing in my spouse and me the ability to think differently toward each other and speak more positively to and about each other. I declare and decree that the atmosphere of our home is changing for the better! I submit myself to Your leadership, Lord, and thank You for revealing my weaknesses to me so that I can turn them into strengths. Help me to be transformed into the very image of Yourself that I might bring glory to Your name. Amen.

ten

SAFEGUARD YOUR MARRIAGE: KEEP ROMANCE ALIVE!

Randy: What happens when people don't realize they need to take measures to safeguard their marriage relationship? The first thing we have to do is learn to deal with imagery versus reality. I may be wrong, but it seems to me that women tend to get more excited about the engagement and the wedding ceremony than the marriage. In other words, they're going for the wedding pictures—the imagery of the perfect wedding—without thinking about the marriage that's following hard on the heels of those lifetime vows.

During all the hullabaloo of shopping for the dress, the flowers, the caterer, and the honeymoon, the reality of life after the honeymoon seems way out there somewhere, locked in a very dense fog! It reminds me of a line from *Gone With the Wind,* "I'll think about that tomorrow."

Paula: The bottom line is—you need a "wake-up call." You must understand that people are imperfect. After you've said "I do," there are jobs to return to, bills to pay, decisions to make, two or more new families to learn to live with . . . and the list goes on and on.

I always say that I can set you free if you'll believe there is no such thing as normal! *Normal* just doesn't exist. Yes, there is a long definition for it in Webster's that says *normal* is "according to, constituting, or not deviating from a norm, rule, or principle; regular; relating to, or characterized by average; an authoritative standard; a model; a set standard of achievement; a pattern or trait taken to be typical in the behavior of a social group."

Here's a reality check: *Normal*, by definition, doesn't exist. Realizing that will set you free. It's frustrating to try to live up to the impossible. You can't possibly achieve something that doesn't exist. So you become frustrated if you try to, and, with regard to marriage, you're in trouble right out of the gates.

Randy: Adam, Eve, Paula, and I were created in the image of God—that means human. You were too. We're all just human. We were redeemed from the sinful nature that would cause us to stray away from our mates and have an affair, for example, but if you are human, there is dysfunction somewhere in you because there is no such thing as normal. In fact, if you think you're normal and everyone else is dysfunctional, you are deceived!

All of us would be so much better off if we'd just take off the labels. Who is to say what is normal . . . what is right? If you viewed this strictly from a cultural perspective, what is normal to a typical American family would be very abnormal to an Asian family. What is normal for a Russian family would be abnormal to an African family.

We've developed some practical tips you can implement to safeguard your marriage from its inception. First, let's define *safeguard,* so we're thinking along the same lines. *Safeguard* means "to protect; defend." Once you've entered into the partnership of marriage—once you've signed on the dotted line—you have to work at protecting and defending the relationship.

You may think some of our suggestions are a little rigid or even legalistic. *Rigid* and *legalistic* are not adjectives ever used to describe Randy and Paula White. In fact, that's a laugh! We're just offering these suggestions based on years of counseling married couples and hearing about the innocent, little things that led to an affair or an unhealthy relationship outside the boundaries. Please take these suggestions seriously. Don't disregard them because they seem so completely unlikely to ever lead you in a direction you think you can't or won't go.

GUARD YOUR HEART

Paula: We must stay on guard against the enemy of our soul. Satan loves to take us down, and he attempts to do that in a variety of subtle, innocent-looking ways. Never put yourself in a vulnerable position, thinking it can't happen to you. Randy always says, "Everyone is just one step away from sin all the time."

"EVERYONE IS JUST
ONE STEP AWAY FROM
SIN ALL THE TIME."

Randy and I don't drive with, eat with, or entertain a member of the opposite sex alone. We haven't made this a policy because we know we'd be tempted to jump into bed with someone. That's not even the issue. But why give opportunity to the enemy?

You may say, "What? Pastor, you've got to be kidding! I work with some wonderful people. I eat out with them every day! We are regularly assigned to conduct meetings, plan projects, or tackle special events together. Naturally, we take breaks, go out to eat, or have meals brought in, but these things would never lead to anything out of the way."

Randy: The most vulnerable position for failure is the thought, "It will never happen to me." You have to develop a line of demarcation so you will know when someone has crossed that line. You know when a flirtation begins to get into your spirit man. You've entertained something, and you begin to notice it.

Watch for flirtation reflected from and directed toward you. Tolerance is usually translated as acceptance and encouragement for that behavior to continue. I firmly believe that every church has Jezebels assigned to it. I believe that my wife plays an important role in identifying those spirits and protecting me, because we men are so blind sometimes.

Don't even try to tell me it can't happen to you, because it can. Remember the incident I mentioned when Paula warned me about the woman who had ideas about a relationship with me via counseling? I didn't see it coming—I'm sorry to say—but faced with this woman in my office alone, there was no doubt that my wife had correctly discerned the situation.

These safeguards I'm talking about don't just apply to ministers. Each of us has certain things in our personal lives that we need to keep a watch over. I do not pick up the opposite sex, for example, and invite them into my car. I just won't do it. Now, if there were a woman pulled over to the side of the road with car trouble and it was raining, I would call a tow truck and wait in my car. I wouldn't let her get into my car. She'd have to stand out in the rain or stay in her car, because she wouldn't be invited into my car.

You may be shocked at that. You may think I sound like an awfully mean guy. It's not being mean—it's just a safeguard. Don't pick up the opposite sex in your car when you are by yourself. Here's a scenario for you—an easy trap to fall into. Someone calls you and says, "My car won't start. Can you give me a ride to the meeting?" Don't go there. Either graciously decline by saying straight out that it wouldn't be something you'd be comfortable doing, or come up with an alternative proposal that involves your spouse or children coming along. Offer to call someone who lives in his or her neighborhood who may be going to the meeting also.

Always be accountable to someone. James Dobson's popular *Focus on the Family* radio program replayed part of a Promise Keeper's rally in which a well-known Christian speaker reiterated safeguarding his relationship to the Lord and to his wife. He said that he has an armor bearer in his life whose task is to always ask him about his relationship with the Lord, his commitment to his wife, the purity of his heart, and whether he lied about any of the previous questions. Accountability is crucial. As a man and woman of God, the enemy knows your potential and has marked you for sin. But you have an Advocate and brothers and sisters in Christ who bear one another's burdens so that you may be healed. Don't open a door for the enemy—run from temptation.

Both Paula and I travel a lot, and people are always trying to shove business cards into our hands—but we don't take phone numbers from the opposite sex. We take someone with us when we travel separately (usually someone on our staff), and anyone who tries to slip a telephone number or business card into our hands is intercepted by our travel companion. There's accountability all the time. What are some of the other safeguards we implement, honey?

Paula: One time when I was traveling, I ran into someone at the airport who I hadn't seen in years and years. Now, this guy was someone I was absolutely in love with when I was in high school. He was my little teenage heartthrob. I always traveled with one lady from the staff, and when I saw this guy and was absolutely sure he was who I thought he was, I said, "See that man over there? I had a relationship with him years ago. He stole my heart way back then. I used to have a real 'thing' for him."

I didn't even walk up to him and say hello. Why open that door? I said to my travel companion, "Let's go to our gate and check in. We need to get out of here." Why did I do that? I wasn't feeling tempted to restart my relationship with him. Absolutely not! There just wasn't any need to open the door of opportunity for any kind of devil to walk through.

Randy: We work hard. Paula traveled more than 300,000 miles last year. From April through November, she was out preaching somewhere in the world almost every single week. That may sound glamorous to you, but it's not, believe me. I traveled for years and years when I started out as an evangelist and associate pastor of a large church in Washington, D.C. I was rarely at home—I was either at the airport, on an airplane, in a hotel, or standing at a pulpit preaching. It gets old mighty quick.

WORK HARD—PLAY HARD

A pastor friend of mine once gave me some very good advice that I will pass on to you. He said, "When you work this hard, Randy, you have to learn to play equally as hard." What does that mean? Paula and I have a date night that is worked into our schedules regardless of what or who else may try to interfere. And I'm telling you to set a date night. We've talked about this previously, I know, but Paula and I enjoy our date nights.

It's an opportunity to separate yourselves from the routine of daily life and be romantic just for the fun of it. Flirt, court, swoon, and keep the fire burning. Do something both of you like to do. Don't include anyone else but your spouse—keep this night like you'd keep the Sabbath, because it's holy. Accept no interruptions. Spend quality time with one another. Look for ways to become involved in something that's really important to your spouse. Keep romance alive!

SEPARATE YOURSELVES FROM THE ROUTINE OF DAILY LIFE AND BE ROMANTIC JUST FOR THE FUN OF IT.

My wife and I have a blast together! We have fun—I mean fun. We act like we are sixteen years old again, and the sky's the limit because she is my partner. We work hard, and when we say we play hard, we do. We don't want to be around the phone, the fax, or the computer. We don't want to deal with church issues and emergencies (although, we would, of course, if something serious came up). This is a time for us to minister to each other.

I take her down to her favorite restaurant or to the mall . . . things like that.

Paula: We do things of common interest together. But let me stress that if you don't set the time—really schedule it and mean it—it will just pass you by. Six months will have passed before you realize it, and you'll feel the absence of your weekly date night in tangible ways. You'll begin thinking things like, *Whatever happened to romance? Whatever happened to courting?* We flirt and do little things that make butterflies fly around in each other's stomach. And this only happens if you *make* it happen.

Mrs. Benny (Suzanne) Hinn taught me this about playing hard. She said after ninety days of hard work, take three days of rest. And that helps me, because I can mentally handle anything for ninety days if I know I'm going to get a three-day break. I can handle an intense time of work—the pressure of the world, the ministry, the building, upcoming crusades, and traveling—if I know it is going to end with three relaxing days alone with my husband.

Our children sacrifice along with us in the ministry, so another thing we do regularly is reward them for all the times we couldn't be where they needed us to be. We'll take them to a special event, check into a nice hotel, and let them see the blessings of God that result from serving Him.

When our children were little, we'd say, "We might have to go without this for now, but it's because there's going to be a future for us." I think that's important. We often forget to enjoy the fruit of our labor. God wants us to have times of rest. He wants us to enjoy the fruit of our labor. Reward yourself, reward your family, and reward your spouse!

Randy: **Do something crazy! When we go out on our date night and see other couples across the restaurant that we know, we duck and head the other way. Now, don't be offended if we've done it to you. It's not that we don't like you, but this is our time to be alone together.**

This just happened to us at the mall. We saw some people who attend our church, and I know they thought we were trying to avoid them. We love people . . . we love these folks we saw, but we knew what would happen. They'd ask us to join them for dinner and a movie. Then our date night would be shot. It isn't that it wouldn't have been fun to do something with them, but the point is—we've set aside this time exclusively to be alone with each other.

So we make it a precedent—nothing or no one will come between us on our date night. We sometimes go to the beach

and neck and French kiss. I mean, we just go crazy and leave imprints in the sand! I keep the fire going. I don't want a little ember glowing once in awhile. I want the fire stirred up in my heart. I can see the headlines now, "Pastor of Without Walls International Church Arrested for Indecent Exposure with His Wife." But she's my wife, I'm in love with her, and I lust after her! Hallelujah!

Continue courting your spouse. Write love notes, bless each other with gifts, whisper sweet nothings into each other's ears, and stare into each other's eyes with longing.

Paula: Now, I've already told you that I had to teach Randy how to be more affectionate, because he just wasn't very demonstrative in that area when we were first married. So you can only imagine what it's like for me to read these suggestions from Randy White about keeping romance alive and safeguarding our marriage. Once he caught on to what I needed from him, he was a quick study. He seldom, if ever, disappoints me in the area of affection and romance now. Love always sees the best in the other person when the flames of romance are constantly stoked.

HARMONY WITH GOD BRINGS HARMONY IN YOUR MARRIAGE

Randy: Build your foundation and keep it strong. Between serving God, raising kids, and paying bills, don't forget that your spouse is the one you will spend the rest of your life with. The last thing you want is to end your life wondering why you have nothing in common. Statistics show that the two most vulnerable years of a marriage are the second and the twenty-sixth! By the twenty-sixth anniversary, the kids are usually out and on their own, and all too often you are looking across the dinner table and wondering, *Who is he (she)? I don't even know him (her).*

Paula: The last thing you want to do is come to the end of your life dancing alone and asking, "Where did we miss it?" Randy referred to the statistic about the twenty-sixth year of marriage being a point of vulnerability. Isn't it weird that people who have been together this long would get divorced?

I think I know the reasons why. The couple stays together for the kids. They build jobs and careers together, but they never take time out for each other. They don't schedule a date night. They forgot to enjoy one another. Like Randy said, they look across the table and think, *We have nothing in common.* I've heard women say, "I don't even know the person I'm sleeping with, and we've been married for a quarter of a century!"

SAVE INTIMACY FOR EACH OTHER

Randy: Don't take each other for granted. We are not promised tomorrow. Live and love today and build a strong tomorrow. Don't forget to express your love for each other at every opportunity. I'll give you a classic example. I was visiting with a man from our church in my office. We had shared some intimate conversation about marriage, family, and life in general.

He had just left my office, hugged me on his way out, and said good-bye. He was going to meet his wife.

I left my office and got into my car. As I drove down the expressway, I noticed a puff of smoke in the air, and then my car phone suddenly rang. My receptionist told me this man's wife and daughter had been killed in an automobile accident that produced the puff of smoke I'd just seen as I drove down the road. I was literally driving right up on the scene of this accident as we spoke. This man had just left my office to meet her, and the next thing he knew, his forty-one-year-old wife was gone.

LIVE AND LOVE TODAY AND BUILD A STRONG TOMORROW.

Never take one another for granted. I don't care how fighting mad you may be at each other, take the time to say, "I love you." That accident that took our friends' lives and just turned their family upside down had a profoundly sobering effect on Paula and me. In fact, go over to your spouse and kiss him or her right now, and say "I love you!"

Paula: Your intimate expression of love needs to come in a way that will be most meaningful to him. I used to go out and buy Randy a suit or something, and I thought I was saying, "I love you" each time I did this. One time Randy told me, "Paula, that doesn't mean anything to me. I want you to do the little things."

I had to start listening more carefully to things he said in passing. They were little clues to direct me to ways he wanted to be shown my love and affection.

Now, for me it was roses. He bought me roses. He bought dresses. He'd buy the moon if he thought it would make me happy. I didn't want that, and I really started resenting his gifts. What I wanted him to do was make time for me. I wanted him to take me to the mall and watch me try on the dress and say, "That one looks good on you." To me, that was saying, "I love you." Find out how your partner receives the message, "I love you."

Save intimacy for each other. There are some things you don't tell your girlfriend or guy friends. Keep your bedroom secrets to yourselves—you know, the little pet names you reserve for each other. Guard each other's secrets. There is nothing more disloyal than telling bedroom or household secrets. This is important, because when a man gives a woman his heart, he's giving her himself.

I've said it before, but it bears repeating—a man can give his body but not give his heart. Don't ever break his confidence. Don't tell your mom. Don't tell your girlfriends. Women chatter in their sharing times. Whenever he shares childhood secrets with you—like the first time he attempted something and was frightened—keep that to yourself. Guard his secrets.

WALK IN CONTINUAL FORGIVENESS

Randy: **Be able to forgive. Nobody is perfect. All of us are striving for perfection, and we forgive as Jesus forgave us. I can truthfully say there is no bitterness or unforgiveness in my heart. I am quick to forgive. Walk in integrity and have a pure heart. Don't carry offenses. I don't care if you've been hurt by what your spouse said—let it go, and let God correct her in His own way and in His perfect timing. If you carry unforgiveness** in your heart, God can't forgive you, and you never want to be in a position where God's hands are tied when it comes to Him forgiving you.

Keep the favor of God raining down on you by forgiving. Revenge will eat you up. It will have you for lunch. Don't document offenses against your spouse in order to have ammunition to use in your next fight.

Paula: Men have egos, and you need to be the one stroking his ego. I think too often we focus on each other's flaws. Don't go there. Don't always be nagging. As Jesus forgave you, forgive your spouse. You're not perfect—nobody is. Go back and remember what you loved about him (her). If you can only find one quality, find it. Search until you find it, and cut him some slack. He needs admiration, not criticism.

I make a point of saying something nice every day as Randy is walking out the door. I say, "You look so good." I just tell him how good he looks no matter what kind of fight or discussion we've had the night before . . . or maybe even fifteen minutes before he heads toward the door. He sometimes says, "I'm a middle-aged, old man. Nobody wants me." I always say, "Every woman in the world would want you, Randy White. You are hot, hot, hot!"

Randy: Help us, Lord! There's not going to be any secrets left untold when we finish this book.

Paula: We're helping people. We're dealing with issues—not textbook stick people who aren't real. Be forgiving. Just overlook some of the things that get on your very last nerve. You can afford it. It doesn't cost a cent to be kind, loving, and generous with truthful compliments and forgiveness to your mate. Forgive and forget it.

Romans 12:16-18 AMP says, *Live in harmony with one another; do not be haughty (snobbish, high-minded, exclusive), but readily adjust yourself to [people, things] and give yourselves to humble tasks. Never overestimate yourself or be wise in your own conceits. Repay no one evil for evil, but take thought for what is honest and proper and noble [aiming to be above reproach] in the sight of everyone. If possible, as far as it depends on you, live at peace with everyone.*

RE-EVALUATE YOUR DREAMS AND GOALS FOR EACH OTHER

Randy: Paula and I do this often. We set goals for each other. Where do we want to be when we are age 50, 60, or 70? Where do we want to be financially? Do we want a house? What kind of car do we want to drive? Set realistic goals together.

We often begin a new year with a list of goals for ourselves, each other, the church, and our kids. Look at your marriage as a corporation that offers a reward or return on the investment you put into it. There's a president, a vice-president, and a board of directors. Make sure everything is in place.

Paula: Randy and I set attainable goals individually and corporately. The operative word is *attainable*. Problems occur in marriage when people's desires remain unmet. What we want, we pursue. Don't make decisions based solely on how you feel at the moment. Emotions can be deceptive.

Pray together during this goal-setting season. Ask God to shed some light on your dreams and desires. Don't be afraid to imagine. The Word does not instruct us to quit imagining but to destroy every imagination or thought that is contrary to God and His will for our lives (see 2 Corinthians 10:5).

FANTASY LIVING CAUSES US TO PUT OFF UNTIL TOMORROW WHAT WE SHOULD DO TODAY.

I totally concur with Randy about being realistic in setting goals. "If only" thinking causes us to procrastinate or put off today's opportunities. A fantasy always awaits the right or perfect occasion. It holds us trapped in a time warp saying, "if only," and waiting for the right time.

James 4:14,15 AMP says, . . . *you do not know [the least thing] about what may happen tomorrow. What is the nature of your life? You are [really] but a wisp of vapor (a puff of smoke, a mist) that is visible for a little while and then disappears [into thin air]. You ought instead to say, If the Lord is willing, we shall live and we shall do this or that [thing].*

Fantasy living causes us to put off until tomorrow what we should do today. We make excuses like—"When the kids are grown . . . when we've saved this much money . . . when we get this or that. . . ." Be realistic, but don't wait too long to see your dreams come true.

TAKE CARE OF YOURSELF

Randy: You cannot love someone else if you don't love yourself. I realize this subject has been an ongoing theme throughout the book, but it cannot be overemphasized. We talked about fitness early in the book—about being physically as well as spiritually fit. It is an important enough issue that we want to go over some of the points again.

You probably didn't marry someone who was unattractive, overweight, sloppy, lazy, and disinterested, but you feel many times every day that you're married to that person now. How did it happen? It happened because he didn't take care of himself and neither did you. Get off the couch, and get on the treadmill. No, it isn't fun, but it's worth it.

In this day and age, there are too many accessible ways to combat most of these physical problems. You simply don't have to let them get out of control. And you can't even use the excuse that diet clubs and plastic surgery are too expensive because, in reality, neither factors into the scenario. Everyone is different, and health issues do contribute to changes in the way we look, but we can still do our best to present an attractive-looking package to our mate.

Paula: Never grow weary of working on the package you present to the world. Ultimately, it is even important to your witness for Christ. Always ask yourself, "What about me would make anyone want to be a Christian?" And if you think looks has nothing to do with that issue, you're mistaken! Why should anyone listen to someone preaching to them who can't even control their eating habits, let alone the myriad of other issues that all of us have to deal with on a daily basis?

GIVE EACH OTHER SPACE

Randy: We're not going to dwell on this issue, because we've talked at length about men needing their space—especially right after they come home from a hard day at work. Give your husband time to unwind, and when he's ready to communicate, he'll let you know. Don't spend your 25,000 to 50,000 words trying to get him to tell you how his day went. He is not interested in using up his 10,000 to 15,000 words a day talking about how things went at work.

Men are directional. They decide what they want to do, what they want to talk about, and when. Give him the space to do that. Remember that a man's worth and value comes from what he does.

One of our associate pastors, my dad, and I recently went hunting. We do men things together several times a year. It's important that we do that without the wives getting upset about it. Women need to get away too. Don't fuss when your wife wants to go to a Women's Conference somewhere, take a trip to visit her parents, or just get together with her girlfriends and spend a weekend shopping and eating out. It's okay to spend some time apart. And it's great fun to renew your acquaintance when you come home! Yeah!

Paula: God made women to be attractive. A wife should work at not being intimidated when her husband looks at another woman and recognizes her beauty. He won't cross the threshold into sin if he's happy and satisfied at home. Recognize that God made you the way you are. It is your responsibility to allow him the space he needs to be who God created him to be.

Husbands need to give their wives some space too. Most men aren't hoverers, but those who are can drive a woman bonkers.

We've talked quite a bit about my travel schedule. When Randy and I have spent too much time together, he usually suggests some place I could go and preach. He sees a trip to the airport in his future. That's okay. It works well for us . . . like the old saying, "I'm happy twice—when they come and when they go." Usually this is said in reference to visiting relatives, but it also applies to our marriage very nicely.

WHAT YOU DO TO CATCH A MAN IS WHAT YOU'LL HAVE TO DO TO KEEP HIM

Randy: **Talk about this, honey.**

Paula: A lot of times, women put the wrong bait on the hook to catch a man. Just remember, what you catch him with is what you have to keep him with. So if you won your spouse with your heart, your tenderness, your caring concern, or your interest in his interests—that's what you'll have to keep him with. What brought you together in the beginning is what's going to make it work in the end.

Here's a bottom-line principle that is especially true of women. When you meet someone, you think you can change that person. You think if you can get him to go with you to church while you're dating, he'll be right next to you in that pew every Sunday morning of your life. Not so if he's only going to church now to impress you. Now, this doesn't mean you can't pull something out of a person, but it has to be in him.

If I'm going to insist on you being something other than who you are, I'm going to frustrate you, and you're going to frustrate me. We can play this game for awhile, but not forever.

BE REALISTIC—
FANTASYLAND IS
OVERCROWDED ALREADY.

When Randy and I got together, I wasn't where I am today emotionally, spiritually, socially, or even physically, but there was something in me. God had put a measure of greatness in me that Randy White could see. He helped develop it in me. He helped pull it out, but he had something to work with. He didn't *change* who I was. He helped *develop* who I was—who God made me to be.

Remember, people change, but not much. Again, be realistic—Fantasyland is overcrowded already.

SERVE AND ENCOURAGE ONE ANOTHER

Randy: **Husbands and wives serve their spouse's needs throughout their married lives. Anyone who goes into the marriage relationship without realizing this will be in trouble, because marriage involves serving one another. Most people have never been** taught or exposed to godly examples of how a man should treat his wife and how a wife should treat her husband.

It's an issue of dual submission. Women don't need to be delivered by joining the feminist movement. Jesus Christ liberated men and women two thousand years ago at Calvary, when He laid down His life for us.

I like what Detroit Bishop Andrew Merritt says, "Christ liberated women and took them back to a place of prominence, positioning them right next to the man. As a result, women's liberation comes to the church in the form of dual submission. The man is to be the leader, the woman is assigned to pray for him so that he will be a good one. The success, happiness, and prosperity of women is tied to their husbands. When you as a wife leave your position as a completer, you will jeopardize your marriage. When you as a husband permit your wife to be neglected, you will likewise put your marriage in jeopardy."

Encourage each other. Harry Truman wrote his wife 1,300 love letters while he served as President of the United States. If the President of the United States, who is running the entire nation, can still write 1,300 love letters to his wife, you need to encourage, edify, and romance your spouse. Words build and words destroy.

Paula: God gave man authority. He gave women influence. The neck still turns the head. Do you get the meaning of that statement? The neck still turns the head. Although the man has authority, the woman's influence turns him in the way he should go. Be an encourager.

I'll give you a prime example. Years ago, there was someone around that I didn't particularly like, and God told me, "Keep your mouth shut to Randy because he's mine before he's yours. And what you say to him will influence how he pastors this person. Don't interfere." I didn't get involved in Randy's association with that person, and God took care of the situation beautifully.

I realized from this incident the power of my influence— that my words carry lots of weight with Randy because God has given me influence on him, and influence directs authority. That's why it's important for wives to pray for their husbands. Understand your role—the two together complete . . . they don't compete. It would be out of order for me to be in authority and Randy to be the influencer. One is not better or less than the other, but understand the two diverse roles. The husband has the role of authority.

I often use that illustration of neck and head when I'm speaking to women, because the neck gives the head direction. The head is still moving, but it's done by the neck. It is vitally important for a woman to understand her responsibility.

Timing is everything. Learn to keep your mouth shut. Learn to control your tongue in the heat of battle. The same words spoken in the right atmosphere will not wound but promote healing. I tell men especially to watch what they say, because women hold things in and remember those words ten years later.

Women need to learn the fruit of the Spirit of self-control. The Holy Spirit lives in you, so you can control that mouth of yours. Words either harm or heal, but timing is important.

PRAY WITH EACH OTHER

Randy: If you want to resolve some difficulties in your marriage, get down on your knees and pray together. Open up before God and your spouse. I challenge you by the power and anointing of the Holy Spirit to hold your spouse and pray with him or her in Jesus' name. Watch the strongholds begin to crumble! Glory to God!

You may not be called to the ministry. You may be a truck driver, work at a bowling alley, or spend your days being the world's greatest mechanic. It doesn't matter what you do—you are the priest of your household. Take your spouse by the hand, or what I typically do is hold my wife in bed and pray, "Lord, just keep us. I thank You for Paula. I thank You, Lord, that she's my help meet. I pray that You will heal her. Keep Your hand upon her. Put Your angels around us tonight."

Paula: When we were dating, I was very intimidated because I thought Randy was so spiritually above me. One night he said, "Paula, I want to pray with you." I just got down on my knees and watched him. I had never seen Randy cry. He's not a crier, but tears just rolled down his cheeks, and he said, "There's never been a woman who prayed with me." I was so touched.

Later, after we were married, one time he prayed, "Lord, make me the husband that Paula needs." That fulfilled me more than anything. It revealed his heart to me. He literally asked God to make him into the man that I needed him to be. It broke down all the boundaries in my life.

I love to hear Randy's prayers over me and our family. We come out of these prayer times feeling like the cartoon character, Popeye, after he's had his can of spinach! The feeling is almost indescribable. It strengthens you for the long haul. Don't deny yourself the strength and resolve that come from praying with your spouse.

If you've never spoken with God in front of your spouse, talk it over first, and go for it a little at a time. Like everything else, the more you do it, the easier it will be. I believe you'll be amazed at the strongholds that come down in your marriage!

MAINTAIN FRESHNESS IN YOUR MARRIAGE

Randy: Invest twenty minutes a day to keep romance fresh in your marriage. Nurture your relationship. Marital happiness fosters intimacy. Every moment that you live, God is scheduling a miracle for your life and sending a deliverer by. All you need to do is be obedient and listen to your spirit, not just to your natural man. Make your spouse number one in your life, and let her (him) know it. Your marriage is your first ministry. Ministry begins at home.

If your marriage has suffered hardship—if it's on the brink of divorce right now—don't give up. Every prison has a door. Every river has a bridge. Every mountain has a tunnel. You just have to find it. God knows where you are. He is touched by the feelings of your infirmities (see Hebrews 4:15).

Paula: It's just a rumor that I always have the last word, but here it is. We need to guard our hearts, because out of the heart flow the issues of life. I love being the queen of Randy White's life. If you're a husband reading this book right now, let me say to you that if you'll just sow into your wife, you're going to reap a great harvest. Be happy when your wife looks good, spoil her, take pride and pleasure in her.

If you're his wife, I say this to you, admire and respect your husband. God gave him to you to protect and defend you, to shelter and care for you. He is a gift for whom you need to be extremely grateful. Give him the very best that you have.

Randy and I hope these little marital lessons we've shared will enhance and bring your relationship up to a higher level. We encourage you to love one another as Christ loves the church. Cherish your relationship with each other—you will never regret the investment you make in your marriage.

May God richly bless you as you seek and serve Him.

Safeguard Your Marriage: Keep Romance Alive!

1. **Guard your heart**
   a. Don't drive, eat with, or entertain a member of the opposite sex alone
   b. The most vulnerable position for failure is thinking, "It will never happen to me"
   c. Be accountable to someone

2. **Harmony with God brings harmony in your marriage**
   a. Build your marriage on the solid rock of Christ Jesus
   b. The two most vulnerable years of marriage are the second and twenty-sixth
   c. Don't come to the end of your life dancing alone and wondering what happened

3. **Save intimacy for each other**
   a. Don't take each other for granted
   b. Express your love for one another at every opportunity
   c. Keep your bedroom and household secrets to yourselves

4. **Walk in continual forgiveness**
   a. Let go of offense, and let God correct that spouse who hurt you
   b. Wives need to stroke the egos of their own husbands
   c. Live in harmony with everyone

5. **Re-evaluate your dreams and goals for each other**
   a. Set realistic, attainable goals
   b. Don't be afraid to dream
   c. Don't let fantasies cause you to put off until tomorrow what you can do today

6. **Take care of yourself**
   a. You cannot love someone else if you don't love yourself
   b. Keep your "package" looking good for your mate

7. **Give each other space**
   a. Give your husband time to unwind
   b. Schedule time to spend apart doing guy things and girl things
   c. Be happy when your spouse takes off with the guys (girls) and be happy when he (she) comes home
8. **What you do to catch a man is what you'll have to do to keep him**
   a. Watch out for the bait you use to hook a man
   b. You can't change anybody—only God can change people
   c. Fantasyland is overpopulated—don't try to move there
9. **Serve and encourage one another**
   a. Marriage requires serving the needs of one another . . . for a lifetime
   b. Dual submission requires a wife praying for her husband, and a husband paying attention to his wife
   c. Harry Truman wrote 1,300 love letters to his wife, Bess. If he can do it, so can you
   d. Timing is critical. Learn the fruit of the Spirit of self-control. Keep still!
10. **Pray with each other**
    a. Men are the priests of their households whether they are called to the ministry or not
    b. If you've never prayed together, try it. Take it slow and get comfortable with it. Your united prayers will tear down the devil's strongholds!
11. **Maintain freshness in your marriage**
    a. Invest twenty minutes a day nurturing your relationship
    b. Don't give up even if your marriage is on the rocks
    c. The last word from Paula

Homework Assignment

1. List ten ways to keep romance alive in your marriage.
2. Sit down together and plan your date nights for the remainder of the year.
3. Spend at least twenty minutes pondering the things that attracted you to your spouse.

Thank You, God, for delivering me from believing there is such a thing as "normal." With Your help, I will do my best to become all that You have created me to be. I ask You to help me to stop comparing my marriage and kids with those I "perceive" to be "normal." Thank You for setting me free in this critical area. Strengthen me, O Lord, in the areas where I have been weak and vulnerable in the past. Thank You for keeping me from opening doors of opportunity presented by the devil to destroy my marriage. Give me creative ideas that will keep the excitement in my marriage—like it was when my spouse and I first met. Help me, Father, to set positive and realistic goals for my marriage, my family, and myself. Thank You for the resolve to commit to praying together that my mate and I may destroy all the enemy's plans for our lives. In Jesus' name. Amen.

Conclusion

MARRIAGE IS HONORABLE

Marriage is honourable in all, and the bed undefiled: but whoremongers and adulterers God will judge.
—HEBREWS 13:4

The Greek translation of the word *honorable* is "holy." The ancient custom of placing pure white linens on the marriage bed stemmed from a desire to prove the sexual purity of a young bride. Blood found on the pure white linen following consummation served as proof that the bride was a virgin and the marriage bed undefiled by fornication.

The blood resulted from penetration of the virgin bride's hymen (the thin piece of skin that covers the opening of the womb) by the male organ during the act of intercourse. So when a man and woman came together for the first time, they literally formed a blood covenant.

That's why when Christians come together as husband and wife in the act of marriage, they are engaging in spiritual warfare.

The blood covenant is powerful and the very foundation upon which our salvation is based. The Israelites practiced the many aspects of the blood covenant through sacrifices as a type and shadow of the blood of our Lord Jesus Christ, whose one-time sacrifice would change the world.

When two become one flesh, it's a powerful union. It is not God's will that unmarried individuals cohabit. You develop a soup time when you become one flesh. For the married couple, that is a healthy relationship ordained by God. For those in fornication, it is an act of sin and disobedience—defying the purpose of marriage.

If you have had previous relationships, the blood of Jesus covers a multitude of sins. It's the blood of Jesus that will set you free. But first you must confess your sins and know that He is faithful and just to forgive you and to cleanse you from all unrighteousness.

So if you did it your way before, God gives you repeated opportunity to repent and turn from your sin to experience the blessing of doing it His way.

Recommended Reading

Dillow, Linda and Pintus, Lorraine. *Intimate Issues: 21 Questions Christian Women Ask About Sex*. Colorado Springs: Waterbrook Press, a division of Random House, Inc., 1999.

Harley, Willard F. Jr. *His Needs Her Needs: Building An Affair-proof Marriage*. Grand Rapids: Fleming H. Revell, A division of Baker Book House Company, 1986, 1994.

LaHaye, Tim. *Spirit-Controlled Temperament*. Wheaton: Tyndale House Publishers, 1993.

Littauer, Florence. *Your Personality Tree*. Nashville: Word Publishing, 1991.

Merritt, Andrew. *The Marriage Enrichment Handbook: Godly Principles for a Successful Marriage*. Detroit: A & V Publishing Company, 1993.

Meyer, Joyce. *Help Me—I'm Married!* Tulsa: Harrison House, Inc., 2000.

Nelson, Tommy. *The Book of Romance: What Solomon Says About Love, Sex, and Intimacy*. Nashville: Thomas Nelson, Inc., 1998.

ABOUT THE AUTHORS

Pastor Randy White is the Senior Pastor and co-founder of Tampa, Florida's Without Walls International Church, recognized as one of the fastest-growing churches in the nation by *Church Growth Today*. Without Walls International Church serves more than 10,000 people in weekly attendance.

Known for his unconventional methods of reaching the lost, Randy brings God's Word to life through sometimes intense, often humorous, and always relevant messages.

Without Walls' multiracial congregation is comprised of rich, poor, and sometimes homeless men, women, and children, corporate professionals, CEOs, and professional athletes all searching for one common thing—restoration—the hallmark of Randy White's career in ministry.

Without Walls' outreaches include over 200 ministries of helps covering a wide range of practical services from a medical clinic to job placement services, drug and alcohol rehabilitation, a community development corporation, a ministerial internship training program, a nursing home, an adoption agency, mobile inner city outreaches, Millennium Generation Youth Ministries, ministries to the homeless and the incarcerated, as well as a successful television ministry.

"Prime Time 20/20" with Diane Sawyer recently visited the church to investigate and report the meaning of speaking in tongues, presenting a positive view of the full gospel in action to a national, secular audience of potentially 9.2 million households.

The author of *Without Walls—God's Blueprint for the 21st Century Church*, Randy White attended Lee University in Cleveland, Tennessee. He holds a bachelor's degree in Bible, a master's degree in divinity, and an honorary doctorate in humane letters.

A well-traveled and popular conference speaker, Paula White is known for her motivational Bible teaching applications relevant to real-life issues of these times. She co-founded Without Walls International Church with her husband in 1991. Under her leadership, many of WWIC's successful outreach programs were established, including a ministry to the underprivileged and at-risk that touches hundreds of families each week.

Paula spearheads *Without Walls International Women of the Word (WOW)*. Her weekly television program, "The Paula White Show," is seen on Black Entertainment Television, which currently reaches 66 million homes. DayStar, Sky Angel, and other markets across the nation also carry her program, reaching a potential viewing audience of more than 35 million.

Paula's book, *He Loves Me, He Loves Me Not,* focuses on helping women see themselves as God sees them. Through her own experiences, she teaches women to see their yesterday as a tomb and their tomorrow as a womb. Her formal education includes work in ministerial studies and Christian education. She has also received an honorary doctorate degree.

The Whites have four children, Bradley, Brandon, Angie, and Kristen, and one grandson, Drew. They reside in Tampa, Florida.

Randy and Paula would love to hear your comments about this book.

Please contact us at:

Without Walls International Church
2511 Without Walls International Place
Tampa, Florida 33607

or visit our Web Site

www.paulawhiteministries.org

Please include your testimony of help received from this book when you write. Your prayer requests are welcome.